Southern
Messenger
Poets

DAVE SMITH, EDITOR

Summer Lake

Summer Lake

new and selected poems

DAVID HUDDLE

Louisiana State University Press
Baton Rouge   1999

Copyright © 1976, 1977, 1978, 1979, 1981, 1983, 1984, 1985, 1987, 1988, 1990, 1991, 1992, 1993, 1994, 1996, 1997, 1998, 1999 by David Huddle

All rights reserved

Manufacture in the United States of America
First printing
00 02 04 06 08 07 05 03 01 99
1 3 5 4 2

Designer: Barbara Neely Bourgoyne
Typeface: Granjon
Typesetter: Coghill Composition Co.
Printer and binder: Edwards Brothers, Incorporated

Library of Congress Cataloging-in-Publication Data

Huddle, David, 1942–
    Summer lake : new and selected poems / David Huddle.
        p.   cm.—(Southern messenger poets)
    ISBN 0-8071-2381-1 (cloth : alk. paper).—ISBN 0-8071-2382-X
(pbk. : alk. paper)
    I. Title.   II. Series.
PS3558.U287S8   1999
811'.54—dc21   99-14899
                                                    CIP

Poems herein have been selected from *Paper Boy* (University of Pittsburgh Press, 1979); *Stopping by Home* (Peregrine Smith Books, 1988); *The Nature of Yearning* (Peregrine Smith Books, 1992); *A David Huddle Reader* (University Press of New England, 1994). The author wishes to thank the editors of the following publications, in which some of the new poems, or versions of them, first appeared: *Atlanta Review, Maine Times, Shenandoah, Slate Run Review, Southern Review.*

"Basket" first appeared in *Introspections: American Poets on One of Their Own Poems*, ed. Robert Pack and Jan Parini, University Press of New England, 1997.

The paper in this book meets the guidelines for permanence and durability of the Committee on Production Guidelines for Book Longevity of the Council on Library Resources. ♾

Nasturtiums and zinnias,
the common flowers,
were what pleased you most,

though for anniversaries
my father gave you red roses,
which you treated like guests

so rich you really didn't
know how to act around them.
You cut lilacs in April—

once I caught you smiling
at a bouquet as if it had told
you something scandalous.

Daffodils made you grieve
they went away so fast,
but irises—now there was

a flower a country girl
could appreciate, pansy
bright, orchid elegant,

determined to multiply.
You were brisk when you tended
your front-porch petunias,

as if they shamed you
with their easy cheer, but
you loved them anyway.

At eighty, dying away
from home, you looked for the red
azalea on the windowsill.

and at thirty, you had a boy
help you tack up kite string
for morning glories to climb.

For Mary Frances Akers Huddle
1919–1999

Contents

from *The Nature of Yearning* (1992)

from *Paper Boy*

(1979)

Town History

J. C. Lawson,
my great-grandfather,
came there poor,
built up a livery
stable, a funeral
parlor, a watch repair
shop, and a general
store. In 1917
when my daddy had sat
in his lap all morning,
my great-grandfather
walked outside,
got shot, and died
that afternoon.
A posse was sent
from Wytheville,
but they didn't catch
Fred Hill until he
gave himself up
the next morning.
My daddy was 7
at the time, and Aunt
Elrica, in her teens,
went into shock
and clasped her hand
over my daddy's mouth
to stop his crying.
She almost smothered
him before he could
get her hand pried
loose.

HOLES COMMENCE FALLING

The lead & zinc company
owned the mineral rights
to the whole town anyway,
and after drilling holes
for 3 or 4 years,
they finally found the right
place and sunk a mine shaft.
We were proud
of all that digging,
even though nobody from
town got hired. They
were going to dig right
under New River and hook up
with the mine at Austinville.
Then people's wells
started drying up just like
somebody'd shut off a faucet,
and holes commenced falling,
big chunks of people's yards
would drop 5 or 6 feet,
houses would shift and crack.
Now and then the company'd
pay out a little money
in damages; they got a truck
to haul water and sell it
to the people whose wells
had dried up, but most
everybody agreed the
situation wasn't
serious.

My Daddy, Whenever
He Went Someplace

Brought gifts
home for me
and my brother
until once the bag
from the 5 & 10
had hammers in it,
which my brother
liked just fine,
took his out
to the back porch
steps, started
driving nails
right away, but
which for some
reason nobody
understands, me
least of all,
offended me,
made me cry
a long time,
and it didn't
take us long
to get used
to the fact
that after that
when he
went someplace
my daddy was
damn sure
coming back
empty-handed.

DELIVERING THE *TIMES*, 1952–1955

80 papers
was all there was
in the whole town,
a 4-mile walk
before school
and 3 dogs
I had to watch out for.
Crow Jim King
broke me in.
He showed me
how to blow snot
out of one side
of my nose holding
the other side shut
with my finger.
In 2 years
I saved $90,
sent off to a Roanoke
pawn shop
for that gold-plated
trumpet Daddy
had to teach me how
to play. And even
though Sunday
was a heavy load,
I walked that route
every day until
I had to start
catching the bus
to the consolidated
high school.

GREGORY'S HOUSE

It was a testimony
to something that
could make my daddy
mad even talking about
it, how when one side
of the house collapsed
they just stopped using
those rooms, and when
the front porch dropped
off Gregory was upset
because he had to do
his drinking in the
kitchen with the kids
whining all around him
and the TV turned up so
loud he couldn't half
concentrate. And they
say when the outhouse
folded over one January
Gregory cut a hole in
the floor and was happy
not to have to make that
trip in cold weather.
But every Saturday
morning they sent out
one dirty-fisted child
to pay me for the paper.
Until that Sunday I
threw a heavy, rolled-up
one too high and up onto
the roof, and it fell
right on through, and
the next Saturday Gregory
himself came out to the

fence and cussed me and
said I owed him damages
for knocking a hole in
his house.

DROWNING

Twin brothers drowned
when I was in fifth grade.
I don't remember who it was
came up the hill to tell us,
but we walked down there
to watch the rescue squad
in boats out dragging
the water with ropes and hooks.
By that time two or three
hundred people were there
beside the river,
clustered and talking.
There had been four of them:
Pete Bushey, Pig Clemons,
and Joe and Charles.
Pete and Pig had made it
to the bank all right,
but the other two, the twins,
were still in the water,
and Joe and Charles always
wore high-top shoes.
They'd broken a lock to get
somebody's old flat-bottomed boat
out to where the current was strong,
and then it had turned over
and sunk on them.
I watched them pull one
and then the other up
out of the brown water
and into the boats.
They had on blue shirts, just alike.
My mother went over
to where the men brought them in
to ask if they were sure

9

nothing could be done
to make them live.
I could hear her voice,
too high,
even over where I stood
with my daddy and my brother.
But they were dead sure enough,
and we walked back
in the hot June afternoon,
my mother stubbing her toe
on a railroad tie
and hurting it bad.

Miss Florence Jackson

Mother said thirty years ago
Miss Jackson had been a handsome
soft-haired girl getting
her certificate from Radford
and coming back home
to teach high-school math.
But I had trouble seeing back
past that loose flesh
that flapped on her arm
when she wrote staccato
on the blackboard.
They moved the high school
twenty miles away to the county seat,
but she stayed there,
taught sixth grade
like a kind of basic training,
and got the boys
to make her new paddles
every time she broke an old one.
James Newman,
drawing pictures of her,
called her "old goose bosom,"
and Bernard Burchett said
she had a voice
like a good sharp hatchet.
Grimmer than God one morning
she told us there would be no more
wrestling matches
between the boys and the girls
during recess,
and that put a permanent
stop to it.
In class I told a joke
my grandaddy had told Peaks
and I hadn't understood

about a cow and a bull
and a preacher,
and she sent me to Mr. Whitt's office.
He made me go back
and tell her I was sorry,
to which she replied
she was too.
Angry in Geography she told
us the explanation for birth control:
"People have a choice
about whether or not
to have children."
They say Miss Jackson
mellowed out
just before she died,
but I was always afraid of her,
everybody was.

Jeep Alley, Emperor of Baseball

Jeep stayed a senior
3 years to pitch ball
because Mr. Whitt was
coach and principal,
but the baseball team
disappeared along with
the high school, and Jeep
was left stranded, just
hanging around the diamond
in warm weather waiting
for us sixth and seventh grade
boys to come play a pick-
up game, cussing us out
for missing grounders or
dropping easy pop-ups.
It flattered us he was
interested because Jeep
weighed better than 200
pounds, always wore his old
blue Yankees cap, and could
fire without even trying
a fastball none of us could
catch. Miss Jackson tried
running him off, but Jeep
treated her like he would
a little thunder shower
that had to be politely
waited out, and we lied for
him because baseball was
the only game any of us
knew how to play, and God
it was good to hear him holler
"Christ Almighty, Burchett,
getcha glove down ina dirt
and keepya god damn eyes
ona ball."

JANIE SWECKER AND ME AND
GONE WITH THE WIND

Janie Swecker had to act
like she wasn't half
as smart as she was
because if she rattled off
the facts fast as she could
think of them, Miss Jackson
would sniff and say, "Well,
Janie, if you're that bored
with the history of your state,
why don't you go back
in the corner and sit
by yourself?"and Janie
hated that because back
there she couldn't get by
with sneaking to read those
library books she loved
while Miss Jackson drilled
the rest of us. So she made
herself talk slow and give
a wrong answer now and then,
and we stopped teasing her
after we understood that
if we hadn't got it done,
she'd do our homework
for us even though she did
C. H. King's and Leo Spraker's
on a regular basis. Janie
let me borrow her mother's
copy of *Gone with the Wind,*
got impatient with me
to finish it but finally
I did and after that in class
sometimes we'd look at each
other and know what we knew.

One night I even dreamed
Miss Jackson was marching
through Georgia,
Atlanta was burning,
and I was riding hard
to pull Janie
out of the flames.

MY BROTHER, BEAUTIFUL SHINAULT, THAT GOAT

My brother and I
always got burnt
in any kind of trade
like once I gave
Gilmer Hyatt half
a stamp collection
for two hamsters,
one fell out
of my pocket
on my way home,
the other one died
two days later,
but the worst was
Beautiful Shinault
getting that year-
old bicycle
off my brother
for a rusted-out
wagon and a goat
that was two-thirds
crazy, which one
day got loose
in the house
and busted up
a chair, five
dinner plates,
a window pane,
two canning jars,
and a screen door,
and after that
Mother said check
with her next
time we got to
feeling commercial-
minded.

What Pig Clemons Told My Mother

She saw him
hunkered down
by the store
over at Porter's Crossroads.
His mouth was gaped open
like it usually was,
and he was staring out
into space with one arm
kind of gangled out
in front of him
like maybe he wanted
a ride but maybe he didn't.
So she stopped the car
—he'd gone to school
with my brother—
and Pig climbed in,
looking gloomy
but polite nevertheless.
My mother,
ever the bright one,
ever the cheerful,
asked him,
"Raymond, where are you going?"
and Pig,
he looked out the window,
away from her,
and told her,
"Aw, Miss Frances,
I'm going to Wytheville
to get drunk,
and God, don't I
dread it."

Mrs. Green

At the screen door
a pretty woman just
married and in shorts
on a Saturday in May,
she was sweet to me
when I came up to collect,
offered me something cold
to drink,
      which I refused
for the sake of dreaming
the whole summer I was
twelve about what it
would be like some
morning to walk
softly into
that lady's
kitchen.

SHOOTING CROWS

Mostly it was starlings
and grackles that landed in
those trees of an evening,
but we called them crows,
and I'd sit out there on
the side of Broomsage Hill,
waiting for Granddad to take
a shot at them, which he
would do two or three times
before it got dark. Now
and then he'd hit one, I'd
watch it fall, tear off over
there under the tree to try
to get a look, once grandly
horrified to see it flapping,
spattering red splotches on
the milkweed leaves, and I
couldn't understand why he
never wanted to see a dead
one, didn't even try all that
hard to hit one, would just
sit there in his khaki work
clothes and smoke one Camel
after another and spit now
and then, try to tease me
about that redheaded Delby
girl I wasn't even slightly
interested in. I liked how
it smelled, though, after he
shot and he'd let me chamber
the fat shells for him. And
once he even let me have a
sip of what he was drinking,

though he cautioned me twice
not to let the old battle ax,
by which he meant my grandmama,
find out about it.

THRESHING WHEAT

My job was to hold the bags
at the end of the chute,
grain sometimes coming down
fast and thick as water.
I grunted to lift those bags,
and Crow Jim'd spit and cuss
me out if I slipped and let
any wheat spill on the ground.
I liked to chew that stuff,
making something somewhere between
chewing gum and bread in my mouth.
One day up in Jim Early's field,
we saw a buck deer, antlers big
as rocking chairs, being chased
by dogs, come out of the woods,
stand still there a minute looking
at the trucks, the tractor, that
house-sized threshing machine,
the men with pitchforks and one
boy scuttering all around.
Then slow as in a dream it
jumped the fence and loped easy
down the hill, the dogs still
yapping back up in the woods.
We all stopped work and hollered
until Peaks told us to get off
our asses and start earning our pay.
In the back of the pickup going
home, we talked about that deer:
Crow Jim swore if he'd had a gun
he'd have shot it, Hitler saying
he'd seen plenty bigger, and Monkey
patting that New Testament he kept

in his top overalls pocket, pulling
me over so close beside him I could
smell the sweat and whispering it
was a sign sent down by God.

EVENING SERVICES EVERY
FOURTH SUNDAY

Dr. Gwathmey came
20 miles
for Mrs. Frye
and just 2 families.
It was funny
Grandmama was
almost too little
to pump anything
on that old organ
except Now the Day
Is Over, with
her glasses slid down
to the tip of her nose
and her mouth all
pursed up tight.
Granddad sat in back,
wouldn't stand
or kneel or pray
or sing but always
too late said Amen
because he'd built
that chapel, then
(for spite Grandmama
said) painted it
his favorite color:
yellow. I had a blue
shirt and wore it
for Toots Pope.
She had black hair
and sometimes stood
beside me outside
in the dark. After
vespers our parents
talked in soft

murmurs, the air
full of cricket
and frog noises,
summer wind,
the smell of
rain coming
later.

My Brother Flies over Low

Nobody could believe
my brother ever got through
that pilot school in Texas
because it was well known
in town he couldn't drive
a car worth a damn. So he'd
made a point of wearing his
uniform whenever he came
home and telling people
to watch out for him, he
was going to fly over low
one of these days. Which
he did, he and a buddy also
stationed down in Goldsboro
made 2 passes, each one sounding
like 14 freight trains
falling off a cliff, waggled
their wings and headed on back
down to North Carolina,
gaining altitude as they went.
Mother was hanging out a wash,
and Mary King was coming up
the hill to help her with
spring cleaning, and they say
Miss Ossie Price came running
out of her store to see what
was the matter. And nobody
sees my brother now but what
they grin at him, shake their
heads, and say something like,
"Great God Almighty, Bill."
Mother won't talk about it
in public, claims to be
embarrassed about the whole
thing, but she doesn't fool
anybody.

GOING, 1960–1970

1

My roommate in Charlottesville
was from Youngstown, Ohio,
a doctor's son, whose parents
took us to Farmington Country
Club and drove me home once
in a Cadillac, first one
except Barnett's hearse
that'd ever been
in our driveway.

2

First airplane
I ever rode was south
to Fort Jackson, South Carolina,
for basic training, but a train
took me north again
to Baltimore, and I was used
to that.

3

Monika Litskus
was a Polish girl I danced with
in Stuttgart bars, and hell,
we might have gotten married
if I'd have known
a language to ask
her in.

4

I took a ferry
from Landau, Denmark,
to Göteborg, Sweden, and there

was tax-free liquor on board
that got all those crazy Swedes
mean drunk and fighting,
and even though that
was on the North Sea,
it reminded me
of home.

5

I spent a Thanksgiving
in Luxembourg City, but it
was raining, so I didn't see
much except a skinned rabbit
and a deer carcass hanging outside
somebody's butcher shop,
and they'd written me
from home that
my grandfather
was sick.

6

I surprised Mother
while she was ironing,
hadn't told anybody I was coming
home on my way west of Hawaii,
wore my khakis and spit-shined
boots over to see Granddad.
He had his shirt off, trying
to shave sitting down
in front of a mirror
He'd cut himself
3 or 4 times he was
shaking so bad.

7

Helicopters
flew me in
to an old cracked
French-built tennis court
near the capital city of
Binh Chanh Province
so that one Asian
could beat up
another one
under my
super-
vision.

8

Drunk on a back street
in Tokyo well after midnight
I was cussed out in perfect English
for something I was only partially
aware of being guilty of by
the most beautiful whore
I'd ever seen.

9

Marines told me
some things they'd done
but in Bangkok I didn't want
to start trading that kind of stories
because, Christ, for $11
you could spend a night
and a day with a woman
you'd dream about years
later.

10

I had a plan
for when I was discharged
of spending the night in the best
hotel San Francisco had to offer
and laying down $100 for some
good-smelling California girl,
but funny thing was I went
straight to the airport
and caught the first
flight home.

11

He was still alive
though they'd kept him off
whiskey all that time, and he
was delighted I'd drive him to
the Wytheville liquor store, where
they spoke to him by name and he bought
five fifths of I. W. Harper, had me carry
the package and hide it in the car trunk,
but even though we met her at the door
and lied we'd been to the optometrist's,
Grandmama found those bottles
before he even got a sip,
went out and on rocks
behind the garage
broke every
god damn
one.

12

In white tie
and tails my father
danced the first two
times in his life, first

with my bride and then with
her mother. There were close
to 300 people watching, and he
kept a smile on his face, got
through it just fine. I felt
like kissing him because I'd
been through enough of a
war to know courage
when I saw it.

13

I was up there
going to Columbia
and drinking cocktails
with writers who knew my name,
but when Mother called
that morning and gave me the news
he'd got up around five,
gone in to pee,
died standing there
(not a joke! not a joke!),
fell wedging his head
between the bathtub and the wall,
my father working
almost an hour getting him out,
knowing all that time
his father was gone,
the only thing I could think
was I have to
get a haircut,
I have to
drive down there,
I have to
go down.

14

It was sunny and cold,
but I didn't feel anything,
I was like something cut
out of a sheet of tin,
and then I saw my father
take off his glasses,
doing what I'd never
in 30 years seen him do,
and swab at his eyes,
and I felt a hurt snap
through my whole body,
wanted just for that instant
to plunge down with him
into that grave, going down
into black dirt, keep going
down with him the rest
of my life.

GIFTS

Plenty of men
already in this family
was Mother's verdict
over news our child
was a daughter.
My father was happy enough
to see that girl baby,
having wondered out loud
several years when we'd get
around to what he called
the main business
of raising children.
He and I talked
about the house
I'd just bought,
or as he put it,
the mortgage I'd signed,
and while my wife
and mother and daughter
were busy doing whatever
it is that two women
and a baby do
upstairs in a bedroom,
he and I went over
across the field to get
some things from Granddad's
old tool shop.
No woman
had ever much cared
for that place
while he was alive,
and the right smells
were still there inside,
the right lack of light,
but the old man's clutter

had been replaced
by an orderliness
he would have found
horrifying.
I looked for the glass
with the dancing girls
who took off their clothes
when you filled it
with water or whiskey,
the naked woman
paperweight,
but they were gone,
and I was outraged
into discoursing
on why the hell
anybody would live
in a place where
people stole
anything of value,
the human condition
was unbearable
enough, even in
civilized towns,
but my father
only half listened
and opened up
a cabinet for me
to get what I'd need.
I took down a wrench,
a saw, some wire pliers,
a couple of screwdrivers.
He picked out
the oldest hammer there,
offered it to me,
and I took it
from his hand.

from *Stopping by Home*
(1988)

TOUR OF DUTY

Nerves

Training I received did not apply
because Cu Chi District was not Fort Jackson.
Funniest thing, they had dogs like any-
where, used them for sandwich meat, I ate one
once, but I guess you want to know if I
ever shot somebody—didn't—would have
—curious about it, but my job gave
one duty, to ask questions. I'd lie

if I said some weren't women, children,
old men; I'd lie too if I claimed these
memories weren't part of my life, but then
shame is natural, wear it, every day
think of bursting from sleep when mortars dropped:
crazy run to a dark hole, damp sandbags.

Theory

Everybody dug a hole and lived in it
when Division first cleared the land near Cu Chi.
Snipers kept the men low a while, but then tents
went up, then big tents. Later, frames of wood, screen-wire
siding, and plywood floors rose under those tents, and that was
called a hooch. Time I got there,
base camp was five square miles of hooches, not
a sniper round was fired in daylight, and good posture

was common. What we wanted was a tin roof.
I was there the day we got the tin to do it with,
blistering hot even that morning we stripped off
the old canvas, took hammers and climbed the rafters
to nail down sheets of tin. Drinking beer afterwards,
we were the sweaty survivors, we were the fit.

Smoke

Base camp smoke was visible fifty klicks
away if you were coming by chopper
up from a three-day pass in Vung Tau or
down past the big mountains near Tay Ninh. Rick
LaTour said the first time he saw it, he
was coming in on the Saigon Express just
at dusk and from the truck it looked pretty.
Rick never said exactly when he first

realized what it was. Explanation
was simple: high water tables meant they
couldn't dig holes; incineration
was logical. Bad duty: to haul those
tubs out from under the outhouses, soak
it with kerosene, let it burn all day.

Work

I am a white, Episcopal-raised, almost
college-educated, North American male.
Sergeant Tri, my interpreter, is engrossed
in questioning our detainee, a small,
bad-smelling man in rags who claims to be
a farmer. I am filling in the blanks
of a form, writing down what Sergeant Tri
tells me. This is dull. Suddenly Tri yanks

our detainee to his feet, slaps him twice
across the bridge of his nose. The farmer
whimpers. Tri says the farmer has lied and waits
for orders. Where I grew up my father
waits at the door while my mother finishes
packing his lunch. I must tell Tri what next.

Bac Ha

As G-5 put it, Bac Ha hamlet was a good
neighbor in 25th Infantry Division's
eyes. Neighbor was a fact, eyes was a lie, and good
was a joke for a fool. Holes in the fence,
paths to the guard shacks, were for Bac Ha whores,
famous for clap, who maybe last year'd worn white
ao dais and ribboned hats to walk the warm
mornings to school, lessons from French-taught priests.

Division's garbage dump was three acres
fenced off from that hamlet's former front yard.
Black-toothed women, children, former farmers
squatted in the shade all day, smiled at the guards,
watched what the trucks dumped out. Walking nights
out there, you'd be under somebody's rifle sights.

Haircut

Open shop on the strip: Vietnamese barber
standing up is not quite as tall as GI
sitting down, but very serious, scampers
around, snips those scissors, raises them high
over GI's head as if GI had hair
longer than a quarter of an inch to start
with and this was a salon in Paris
instead of a shack with no walls and a dirt

floor. At the end he carefully clips hairs
from GI's nose, inserts two small hollow
bamboo sticks in GI's ears, twists them on each
side to ream out the wax, then twangs the sticks. Holds
GI's head, limbers the neck, pops it, scares
GI. Could have died then. 25 p. please.

Beer

Had to send to Saigon for it and what
they sent us was what we got. Sometimes Miller
High Life, Bud, or Black Label, but oh shit!
there was that cheap Australian killer
beer, Swan Lager, God forbid a truckload
of that stuff, it would last for weeks. Better
than no beer, red-haired Leroy always said
when he passed you a can, Leroy getting fatter

by the day sitting behind that bar. Well,
he had a point, because once the truck came back
with not a goddamn thing but two billion
cans of apricot nectar. We saw hell
clearly that day. Apricot nectar! Soon
all of us were out there staring at that truck.

R&R

Out of Tan Son Nhut flying to Bangkok
on a Pan Am 707 a stewardess
handed out iced-down washcloths, using tongs
to offer them from her tray down to us.
Think about a planeload of soldiers
washing their faces and falling in love,
grunts from the field who'd sweated out their own
deaths for months of nights, administrative

types like me whose days were spent trying
not to drip sweat on reports we'd just typed
up for Captain Kiss My Ass. In Bangkok
I spent three hundred dollars, on women
mostly—don't regret a dime—but what I've kept
is Miss Moore, handing me my cool white cloth.

Words

What did those girls say when you walked the strip
of tin-shack bars, gewgaw stores, barber shops,
laundries, and restaurants, most all of which
had beds in back, those girls who had to get up
in Saigon before dawn to catch their rides to Cu Chi,
packed ten to a Lambretta, chattering, happy
in their own lovely tongue, on the dusty
circus road to work, but then what did they say?

Come here, talk to me, you handsome, GI,
I miss you, I love you too much, you want
short time, go in back, I don't care, I want
your baby, sorry about that, GI,
you number ten. A history away
I translate dumbly what those girls would say.

Them

Sergeant Dieu, frail Vietnamese man,
once sat down with me, shirtless, on my bunk
and most astonishingly in my opinion
(not his) squeezed a pimple on my back.
My first trip to the field, I saw Vietnamese
infantry troops, loaded with combat gear,
walking the paddy dikes and holding hands.
I was new then. I thought they were queer.

Co Ngoc at the California Laundry
wouldn't say any of our words, but she
explained anyway a Vietnamese treatment
for sore throat: over where it's sore inside
you rub outside until that hurts too. That
way won't work for American pain. I've tried.

Cousin

for John H. Kent, Jr., 1919–1982

I grew up staring at the picture of him:
oak leaves on his shoulders, crossed rifles
on his lapels, and down his chest so many medals
the camera lost them. He wore gold-rimmed
glasses, smiled, joked about fear. He told true
stories that were like movies on our front porch:
he'd fought a German hand to hand. The word
courage meant Uncle Jack in World War II.

Ten years from my war, thirty from his, we
hit a summer visit together; again
the stories came. He remembered names of his men,
little French towns, a line of trees. I could see
his better than mine. He'd known Hemingway!
I tried hard but couldn't find a thing to say.

Vermont

I'm forty-six. I was twenty-three then.
I'm here with what I've dreamed or remembered.
In the Grand Hotel in Vung Tau one weekend
I spent some time with the most delicate
sixteen-year-old girl who ever delivered
casual heartbreak to a moon-eyed GI.
I am trying to make it balance, but I
can't. Believe me, I've weighed it out:

rising that morning up to the cool air where
the green land moved in its own dream down there,
and I was seeing, the whole flight back to Cu Chi,
a girl turning her elegant face away
after I'd said all I had to say.
This was in Viet Nam. Who didn't love me.

ALBUM

Music

Their white duck trousers, their dark coats, their grave
faces give us out here in the future
to understand such dignity was no
small matter. They surround two demure
women in long dresses, the best piano
players in town. The men hold instruments they've
just started making payments on, their large hands
cradling the horns. Most players of this band,
formally seated here, are carbide men who might
in two hours be shoveling gray dust: trumpet,
trombone, clarinet, tenor saxophone.
The one standing, holding his alto like that,
is my jaunty father, whose music I've known
all my life from this silent black-and-white.

The Field

The breeze stops, the afternoon heat rises,
and she hears his back porch screen door slap shut.
She sits still, lets her mind follow him through
the swinging gate into the field, his shirt
and white flannel pants freshly pressed, his new
racquet held so loosely that it balances
exactly in his hand. Now my father
takes the stile in two steps. And now my mother
turns in the lawn chair, allows herself the sight
of him lifting the racquet as if to
keep it dry. This instant, before he comes
to where she sits under the trees, these two
can choose whatever lives they want, but from
the next it is fixed in shadow and light.

The House

White clapboard, of course, but it's of the stained wood
of the stairwell I think first, light slanting
down from the high window at the turn, dust
motes floating for the nap-bound boy standing
with his foot stopped on the first step. He must,
he knows, pass up through shadow to his bed,
but now he's still as light itself. Mother,
he knows you grew up here, too, and Mother,
what's stalled him out here, banister-handed
and knee-bent, is that sight that came to him
from watching that shaft of the afternoon sun
from the high window at the turn. The dim
shape in front of him is a small girl: one
day you stopped here, this way. He's astounded.

Two Facts

My mother married when she was fifteen.
Her first child, a girl, lived only minutes.
My father, discussing religion with me,
said he'd "had a hard time" in his twenties.
I think about them. Stopped in reverie
I've held in mind this tableau, this scene:
Faith lost, he sits beside her on the bed.
No child now, she can think only of the dead
child who would have been my older sister.
Though I never saw them so young, I know
how their faces look there, the light falling
in slats into that upstairs bedroom. I know
some of it. But I am afraid of feeling
how much they ache to say daughter, daughter.

The Front Yard

The main difference between yard and lawn
is a yard has crabgrass, dandelions, holes,
bumps, and ruts, while a lawn is smooth. In ours, moles
made sure what we had was a yard. Mother
desired a lawn, though, and called it that. Her
lilacs and forsythia dreamed along
with her, but honeysuckle grew over
our fence, up our porch lattice, and clover—
better for us than for the farmers it bloomed.
Ours was a yard all right. Now I ease
the dark and cold of this northern winter:
I dream a boy with a mason jar for bees,
both honey and bumble, hummingbirds never captured,
and lightning bugs for when it's late in my dark room.

Porches

Our front porch faces back toward the road,
the railroad tracks, and the river. A field
of scrub cedars and broom sage holds a path
up which once Crocketts drove their '53
Chrysler, directed by a roadside drunk (half
for fun and half for spite), which episode
showed, though formal callers walk around, our back's
our front—cars come there—and our front's our back,
so that most visitors on a summer day
step up on a damp concrete slab just hosed down,
walk past a cellar door with a hole in it
for the cats, enter the pantry—by now
Mother's face burns—and they all try to fit
in the kitchen and wish they'd come the other way.

Groceries in the Front Seat

I ask Mother if I can look at the road,
she says yes, and so I open the door
and swing out as far as I can, watching
the blur of our driveway gravel, much more
interesting the closer I get to it. Catching
my belt, Charles asks Mother to stop, in this bored
tone of voice. When she glances back, she screams,
slams on the brakes, switches off the engine, leans
her head on the steering wheel for a while
before she slowly drives the rest of the way
home. She's almost seen her baby crushed.
Charles picks up his comic book, finds his place,
and ignores the looks I give him for having rushed
my contemplation of moving gravel.

A History of the Pets

Butch, a black cocker spaniel, collected
stinks, dirt, and open wounds into which our
father poured gentian violet. Did not
come back one morning. A brown-and-white mutt
—I don't recall its name—was shot by our
mother, beheaded, and pronounced rabid
by health folks who provided all five of us
with fourteen Friday nights of shots. There was
Hooker, half-Persian cat who'd claw your back-
side through the open-backed kitchen chairs and swing
by his hooks till you pulled him loose. Rabbits.
Small possums loose in the house. Short-Circuit,
affectionate cat that walked crooked, that'd been
BB-shot in the head. Goat. Skunk. Some snakes.

Dr. Zeno's Laboratory

Dr. Zeno's Private Laboratory /
Keep Out / Genius at Work was the sign
Charles hung on the hitherto entirely
uninteresting back-room door, which sign
transformed a storage space into nearly
the most desirable territory
I have ever been denied access to,
through which door I heard *Eureka! Presto!*
and *Caramba*! from the place outside where
I stood many minutes hoping he'd let
me in. He did not, though now and then he
stuck his face out, eyebrows raised. Nor did he forget
and let slip the Secret. I'm well past forty;
I still wonder what the hell he did in there.

The School

On one side the high school, on the other
grades one through seven, the purple-curtained
auditorium shrank and grew shabbier
each August we came back. Mr. Whitt one year
decided Charles Tomlinson, Slick King, Dwayne
Burchett, Bobby Peaks, and Big Face Cather
could be a basketball team. They practiced
on a rocky, red-dirt court with a basket
and some boards on a post. They drove to games
—always at the other school—in Slick's Ford.
Uniforms were jeans and T-shirts. Big Face
and Bobby played barefoot. They lost by scores
like ten to ninety-three, unaccustomed to such space,
wooden floors, lights, adults calling them names.

Croquet

This decorous, nineteenth-century
entertainment my Newbern grandmother
and great-aunts come down from front-porch rocking chairs
to play an afternoon hot enough to smother
Methodist ladies who say their prayers
at night but who roquet in quiet fury:
Gran gathers her concentration, pauses,
then lets her red mallet fly forth, causes
her skirt to follow her follow-through, then sweeps
it down and follows her red ball. Two wicked
split shots Aunt Iva fires. Aunt Stella, bones
skewed by childhood polio, makes wicket
after wicket, strikes the post, and in dining-room tones
says, "Keep your manners but play for keeps."

Icicle

I smacked you in the mouth for no good reason
except that the icicle had broken off
so easily and that it felt like a club
in my hand, and so I swung it, the soft
pad of your lower lip sprouting a drop,
then gushing a trail onto the snow even
though we both squeezed the place with our fingers.
I'd give a lot not to be the swinger
of that icicle. I'd like another
morning just like that, cold, windy, and bright
as Russia, your glasses fogging up, your face
turning to me again. I tell you I might
help both our lives by changing that act to this,
by handing you the ice, a gift, my brother.

Kitchen Tables

There were two, small one replacing large one
after Charles and I went to Charlottesville
and left them having meals with only three
to sit down, or sometimes just two because Bill,
with Jim Pope, was out courting catastrophe
in their Dodge or the Popes' Ford, oblivion
turned up high on the radio, Pabst cans
cooling their thighs, both those boys in the trance
of a warm summer night when you're able
—our parents had one daughter who died, three
sons who were always leaving for somewhere—
to race toward some girl's house on county
roads that billow up dust behind you while your
mother and father sit at a small, round table.

Sunday Dinner

If the whole length of the white tableclothed
table my grandparents called each other
Old Devil, Battle Ax, Bastard, and Bitch,
if having stopped smoking for Lent, Mother
was in a pout, if New Deal politics
had my father telling us how much he loathed
Roosevelt, if Grandma Lawson's notion
that we boys needed a dose of worm potion
had Charles trying hard not to look amused
and Bill whining for dessert even though
he hadn't finished his beets, if all this
and Uncle Lawrence's thick White Owl smoke,
Aunt Elrica's hoots, and Inez's craziness
weren't my one truth, I'd ask to be excused.

Coda

Sons grown and gone, they adopt a mutt
that comes, stays ten years, and learns their ways.
On slow walks that good dog leads my parents
a hundred yards out the gravel driveway
until a gunshot rips through one day's silence.
My mother and father break into a trot,
though they are old now, too old to run like
this to the curve of the road and the sight
of fat old Daisy's neck a bloody spout,
one spent shell a step away, smoke still spooling,
the backs of two running boys, the one not
carrying the gun looking back and laughing.
They are not strong enough to lift the weight
of their dog. They turn back to the empty house.

Through the hundreds of miles between my house
and theirs, my daughters, my wife, and I
take turns talking with my parents in our
twice-a-month phone call. In our talk we try
to pretend it won't be long before our
visit next summer. I hardly hear how
their words sound; I've lost them and they've lost me,
this is just habit, blood, and memory.
They pause, then they tell us about Daisy,
how she must have walked right up to those boys
before they shot her down. . . . And yes, I am
seeing just how it was. My mother's voice
breaks. I am with you, I want to tell them,
but I manage to say only that I see.

Stopping by Home

Five times since July my father
has been hospitalized. He's home
today, sitting up at his desk
in bathrobe, pajamas, slippers.
I am embarrassed, I want him
fat again, in khakis that smell
like sweat, cigarette smoke, carbide,

ignoring me because he'd rather
work the crossword puzzle, alone
or pretending to be, than risk
in those minutes before supper
finding out what meanness I'd been
up to. He's thin now. And pale.
Waiting to hear what's on my mind.

—⁂—

In the summer in the hospital
he sat on the bed's edge clutching
that Formica table they crank up
and put your food tray on. He coughed
up white mucus, took oxygen
from a thin green tube, couldn't sleep,
couldn't lie back and breathe. He

and my mother thought it was all
finished the day he got medicine
to make him relax, make him sleep,
then couldn't sit up because he'd lost
his strength but couldn't breathe lying
back. They rang for the nurse, but he
passed through something you couldn't see.

They say his hair turned white. It's true,
it's grayer than it was, almost
white. He can't read much now, has no
power of concentration, mind
strays. Today he talks about friends
who've died, relatives long gone.
In a photograph he points out

which ones are dead now. "But you
and Lester Waller and Tom Pope
and George Schreiber and James Payne—so
many still alive," I remind
him. He seems not to hear and bends
to put the picture away. "Some
still around," he says, "yes, no doubt."

—⁕—

My mother wants us to talk. This
is what she always wants, her sons
sitting around with their dad, talk
being evidence of love, she
thinks. My evenings home from school,
the army, New York, or Vermont,
she'd leave the room for us to do it.

We always argued politics.
Didn't intend to, but reasons
came to us. Once he said I ought
to go to Russia and see
how what I'd just said was pure bull,
and I walked out. Words are too hard
for us now. We'll just have to sit.

—※—

Their lives in that house before he got too sick must have been
so filled with silence that even when a truck would pass
on the highway down the hill they would listen. Those
clear sunny days of May and June she sat with him
on the front porch where sometimes the soft wind
rustled in that hackberry that's grown
so high now. I hold an infant

recollection of the sun
warming the three of us,
their holding me so
close between them
I knew then
what home
meant.

So
if I
care so much
about them I
have to sit up here
a thousand miles away
and write myself back home, why

not look for a job down there, try
to find some town close enough to say,
"I'm going to see them," drive over there
and walk in the door and not even surprise
them, sit down with them and talk, maybe stay for lunch,
say an easy good-bye and leave without feeling like
I betrayed them, and I will never find my way back home.

Night comes down, the winter sky
momentarily ecstatic,
then stunned, bruised, ruined with pain, dark. . . .
Coal on the fire, our old habits
keep us still, without lights, sitting
until the study's bay window
yields maybe one moving tree branch.

Then Mother rises, breathes a sigh
for all three of us when she flicks
on the overhead light. The dog barks
lightly in its sleep. We blink. It's
not late. His fingers shake setting
his watch. Before us are the slow
hours, each breath he takes a chance.

At six we move from the study
to the living room for the news,
the weather report our excuse.
The man draws snow over the whole
Northeast, freely uses the word
blizzard, and I stand up before
he's finished and say I think I

better keep driving north, maybe
I can beat that storm. "But son, you
just got here." Mother's hurt. He's used
to my skedaddling ways, and so
makes himself grin, offers his hand
for me to shake, and at the door
we say our word for love. Good-bye.

—⚮—

I scuttle out into the dark
and drive three hundred miles north, numb,
knowing that I hurt but not able
to register it, a busted
speedometer on a car that
hurtles forward. In the morning
I get what's coming to me. Snow

starts in Pennsylvania, slick
stuff on those mountains south of Scranton,
the interstate a long white table
of ice, everything blasted
white. Wind and drifts in those high flat
stretches near nowhere. Endless dream
of losing control, moving through snow.

—⚮—

Tell me whose parents don't get old.
Your father's sick, and you can't stand
to be around him and help him
die or get well, whichever it
turns out he's going to do. Well,
son, you deserve to drive through snow,
wind and freezing cold, past Hometown,

Port Jervis, Newburgh, Kingston. No
decent motel would have you, can't
stop, can't give your old man an arm
to help him walk into the next
room. Albany says go to hell,
keep driving, boy, get your ass home
where you've got children of your own.

Things I Know, Things I Don't

—⚬—

Virginia in early October
is a soft countryside, color not yet
in the trees but the leaves' green going pale,
the sunlight's angle sharp, the birds about
to move. Those cool mornings you catch a whiff
of woodsmoke, evenings you feel a chill
ring the air like a high, soft-blown flute note.
That season of my father's death was not
wrong, not wrong at all. If he had been well
that day he might have taken a walk with
Mother, one of their short strolls. Early that
morning there'd been heavy fog that was all
gone by nine. He'd have liked how that sun felt
on his shoulders. He'd have liked that weather.

—⚬—

Wytheville Hospital, February, 1985

To help his cracked rib heal, he was supposed
to wear a rib-brace with a Velcro seam.
Charles and I hadn't seen him so confused

(though one night at home he'd made Charles let him lean
on him while he urinated from his upstairs
bedroom window, thanked Charles nicely when the stream

ended, then went back to bed). Anyway, there
we'd driven a thousand miles to his bedside
and our assignment was to make him wear

this corset he'd want loose and then decide
it wasn't tight enough, and he got the word
Velcro on his mind, would say it every five

seconds, "Get this Velcro fixed, Dave," or weird
things like, "I gotta go to Velcro now."
About the sixty-seventh time I'd heard

"Fix the Velcro, Dave," I gave him a scowl
and told him I guessed he could live with it
the way it was. It was late, I was out

of patience, having been his good servant
all afternoon. (Charles would take the morning
shift.) Hallway noise made the room seem quiet,

and the blank, beige wall was occupying
his attention like a text he was about
to be quizzed on. But then he was eyeing

me in that sideways way of his, and out
of the corner of his mouth, he said, "If
I were a little stronger, I'd kick your butt."

I wish I could say I stuffed a handkerchief
in my mouth, but for most of my life we'd
been arguing. "You could fix it yourself,

if you were a little stronger," I said,
and he said yes, he guessed that was the truth.
Not much dialogue after that. He faded

back to talking with dead Uncle Jack, with
men who'd worked for him at the carbide plant.
He called me Charles or Bill, let loose a hoot

now and then, "Velcro, Velcro!" or "I want,
the urinal!" or once just "Wee-wee, wee-wee!"
and I'd help him with that, though it wasn't

ever more than a drop or two. Easy,
after a while, waiting on him that way,
when I had dreaded it so intensely

I thought I'd freeze up if I had to stay
with him an hour by myself. That night,
driving his car out on the interstate,

I imagined Mother driving him there right
after he'd taken the fall that broke his rib.
She'd just finished lecturing him about

not doing enough for himself, when he slipped
trying to stand up and fell against a chair
right in front of her eyes. Ashamed, mad, scared,

she must have known more then about despair
than I'd learn in my lifetime. We'd lost count
of his trips to the hospital that year

and the year before. Almost always he got
worse, they sent him home hinting that he'd die
soon, but then somehow he'd improve and astound

us all. Without seeming to try, he survived.
It wasn't the man's will to live; it was
his fear of dying, I thought, but then I'd

always judged him harshly. Next morning Charles
and Mother questioned me all through breakfast.
I told about the Velcro, but as far as

I was concerned, the butt-kicking lambaste
and what I'd said were my business. Charles said
when he'd teased him yesterday, Dad had asked

him to please stop the cutting up. "Ah, God,
Charles," he'd groaned, "you have cut up so damn much!"
The way we laughed then made it seem not so bad,

though of course things were terrible, he in such
relentless misery, Mother depressed
and exhausted, Charles and I good for just

a few days of help, when it was endless:
for years he was going to be running
up to death and out over the abyss

like the *Roadrunner* coyote, cunning
in spite of himself, clawing his way back
to life after we'd all given up on him.

We didn't then, at breakfast, or in fact
ever, acknowledge what was obvious:
if he got better, another attack

would come in a few months, and they got worse
each time. If he got better, we had it all
to go through again. "And what about us!"

I might have yelped, but I wanted my small
soul out of sight. What I meant was Me! What
about me? I hated the hospital,

hated my father's dying the way I'd hate
to sit still, listening to someone's soft,
constant weeping, someone I couldn't

help at all. That morning I read half
of Susan Cheever's *Home Before Dark,* her
memoir of her troubled father enough

to make me forget mine. It was Cheever
I thought about that afternoon, driving
back to the hospital to take my turn

again. When I walked in, Charles was smiling
as if our sleeping father had told a joke
he wanted to tell me, he was spinning

me around to the door, pushing me back
into the hallway. We leaned on the wall.
"Wee-wee! Wee-wee!" he whispered in a croak,

but you laugh softly in a hospital
if you laugh at all. When Charles left, I walked
back in and sat down. My father was still

asleep; his breathing pulled his neck-cords taut,
then let them loose. I had to will myself
not to sit and gape while his body fought

to keep the life in him. I'd think, what if
this is his last breath, what if he dies now,
this instant, while I'm watching? Then he'd shift

a leg or cough or rub his nose, and I'd know
he was miles from death and call myself a fool.
John Cheever was gravely ill but somehow

managing to keep himself witty, cool,
decorous, and brave, snubbing his cancer,
bearing his pain. Achieving a final

dignity seemed to be Cheever's answer
to his years of drunken ignominy.
My father had to wear adult Pampers,

had to be spoon-fed, his exemplary
sober lifetime having earned him the right
to have his sons treat him like a baby.

I looked up and saw his face in the light,
looking right at me but with his eyes glazed.
I doubted he knew me. In this polite

voice he said, "Dave," and swallowed and said,
"I want to go home." I said, "Well, I know
you do." He held my eye, and time passed

like a stopped train. "To Ivanhoe,"
he said as if I didn't know that sorry
town where we'd all grown up, that cruel joke

of a town so poor, so mean, and so ugly
that all you had to do was say the name
in Wytheville and somebody would swear he

almost got killed there one night. But right then
I knew what he had in mind, long summer
days, afternoons turning cool, croquet games

until full dark. "Ivanhoe," he murmured,
"Ivanhoe, sweet Ivanhoe." He was quiet
then, holding it in his mind; then he stirred

his legs, threshed his arms, asked me goddamnit
what was I waiting for, go get the car
and pull it up to the door—he pointed

toward the hallway—he'd meet me right there.
I explained about how when he got well
we'd take him home, we'd take him anywhere

he wanted to go, we'd take him— "Ah, hell,
son," he said. Then it was as if he hung
up the phone on me and let himself fall

into confusion and delirium.
He picked at the sheets and spoke to a man
who had apparently emerged from the ceiling,

asking my father for money. I can
take just so much craziness. I read hard:
Cheever's family gathered around him;

the minister had trouble in the dark
bedroom reading the last rites, ". . . thy servant,
John." They said the Lord's Prayer, then John's heart

stopped. "It was so fast, it was so fast," wrote
Susan. I looked up and watched my father's slow,
demented gaze sweep the room, saw him point

toward that place in the ceiling as though
he'd just driven away his enemy.
He'd lost so much weight that he seemed more bone

than flesh. . . . Here was some old geek claiming he
was the same man who'd showed me how to blow
soap bubbles in the bathtub, how to read

music, how to drive a car, showed me how
trying to be honest, work hard, and raise
a family was one way you could go

to bed at night and get some sleep. Here was
this babbling monster who'd stolen the life
my father made with thirty thousand days

of labor and decency. Now here it
pointed to the light, it made a quick stab,
it lurched in its bed and swung its arm as if

battling something invisible. "Want," it said.
Would it ever stop goddamn wanting? "On,"
it moaned. "No!" I rasped at it. I was mad

enough to walk out. "You need a light on
to read," my father said. "Turn it on, son."

—〰—

Harmonicas kept turning up in desk drawers,
filing cabinets, and attic boxes—
weathered rectangular boxes with pictures
of German marching bands on the lids; inside

they were shining metal with a brassy smell.
Exploring his stuff, my brothers and I
dug them out of places he'd stashed them.
Sometimes he'd take an interest in one

that hadn't made a sound for twenty years.
This would be while he sat at his desk
with a boy at each elbow, another at his knee.
He'd cup the harmonica in both hands and blow

a few notes. Always he stopped and looked
away from us boys there waiting for him
to go on with "The Black Hawk Waltz," "Little
Redwing," or "She'll Be Coming Round the Mountain."

—〰—

He hit me once
                lightly
when I was cutting up in the bathtub
with one of my brothers. I do not
remember the hit.
                I remember
splashing the warm water,
the white tub all around,
him sitting above it,
wiping off his glasses,
not laughing
anymore.

—∞—

To court my mother he walked over to her house to play tennis
with her and my Aunt Murrell. There must have been a fourth,
but I don't know who that was. It must have started when she
was around thirteen, when he'd recovered from rheumatic fever
and instead of going back to Emory & Henry to finish a degree
in physics he'd gone to work for his father at the sand plant
mostly because grandmama couldn't stand the idea of his going
away and getting sick again. His features were delicate; his
tennis whites set off his skin, sun-darkened that summer from
their daily games; he was tall and thin and had good manners;
he played all sorts of musical instruments; he read magazines
and books mother had never heard of; and on the tennis court,
he was both a gentleman and a fine athlete. When it got dark
I'm sure she had to go inside, but twilights last hundreds of
years up there where she lived, and the fireflies come out in
that first cool air that prickles the skin of your arm. When
old full dark came slowly down, he said, "Your white dress is
holding all the light." Her older sister walked indoors, and
that faceless fourth rode a rickety old bike out the driveway
and out of their memories forever, but still they stood there
talking about shooting stars. The miracle of it is that they
waited two more years before marrying. Whenever they told us
about their tennis, they made it clear they both played well.

—⚞—

"Duck-footed,"
Monkey said,
"is how you
Huddles walk,"
the occasion
for Monkey's
observation
being his and my
walking from
the barn to
somewhere and
seeing Charles
walking from
somewhere else
toward the barn,
when Monkey,
who'd started
school with our
father but hadn't
gotten further
than about fifth
grade when he
quit, Monkey
who in most
circumstances
was kindness
incarnate, but
who suffered
the failing
of the truly
ignorant, the
inability to
see other than
accurately, said,
"Look at that boy
walk, walks just

like your daddy,"
and I, whose
IQ was already
several points
higher than his
even though my
head came to
just about his
belt, I who
would attend
fourteen more
years of school
than he and who
had already
taken to spending
as many hours
every day staring
into a mirror
as Monkey did
praying and he
prayed a lot, I who
had this vision
of myself as an
amalgamation
of a cowboy movie
star, a Cleveland
Indians pitcher,
and a benign
millionaire,
asked him, "How's
that, Monkey?"
and he said,
"Duck-footed,
honey, don't you
know all you
Huddles walk
that way?" and I
said, "I don't,"

and he glanced
at me and said,
"That's just because
you're making your
feet stay straight,"
then looked at me
again and laughed
and went on to say,
"Honey, it's nothing
to be ashamed of.
All you Huddles
walk kind of
duck-footed."

—⁂—

Christmas vacation of 1960, my first year at the University of
    Virginia,
we were up late talking and I asked my father (because my best
    friend
from the dorm had confided in me that he was one) what he knew
about homosexuals, and my father said nothing, said he didn't
know a thing, and do you know what he did? (This will tell
you everything you need to know about the time
and the place I grew up in and the kind
of family we were.) My father
got out the dictionary
and looked
that word
up.

—⚯—

Because you see books was what
they put their faith in,
my father and my grandfather,
what they turned to when

they hit something they didn't
know about and wanted to,
or any kind of problem, like how
you dug post-holes, how you

stored apples, or covered a cistern.
My grandfather taught
himself veterinary medicine,
chemistry (he also bought

all the stuff you needed
to practice these things—tools,
equipment, drugs, machinery,
chemicals, cabinets, and scales),

learned watch repairing,
welding, farming, plumbing, carpentry,
bee- and orchard-keeping, oil-painting.
That man would try

anything, and everything meant
a set of books, his proudest
possession the five shelves
of volumes that meant he'd finished

the International Correspondence School
course of instruction
in civil engineering. His income
matched the multiplication

of his interests for a while,
and his house was headquarters
of Charlie Huddle's Empire,
my father his somewhat smarter

but less imaginative assistant.
Nowadays we know the history
of empires. My grandfather lived
to see his machinery

auctioned off, but even then
he and my father pored over
books, calculating what to hold
on to, hoping to discover

the key to preserving what
they'd built up. If charts
existed, they'd probably show
1950 as my grandfather's

last good year, though the downward
curve would be a slow slide.
And though Hiroshima and Nagasaki
were on the opposite side

of their globe, he and my father
understood the men who made
the bomb, men of science, men
who solved problems, who read

books and figured out how
to stop a war. The family line
was that Roosevelt and the New
Deal caused the decline

in our fortune. So when I moved
to New York City to attend
Columbia and once wrote out
for my father a passage I found

in the *New York Times Book Review*,
something Buckminster Fuller
said about work being one
of the silliest human activities ever

invented, I was carrying out a tradition
of digging wisdom out
of books and sharing it with my kin.
When he sent back a quote

from William Henry Hudson that said
(and here I must paraphrase
from memory), "Sir, I cannot help
but recognize what is false

when I directly encounter it,"
my ears burned, but I could see
him checking through our bookshelves
for Hudson, William Henry,

and hoping he could find those words
he only dimly remembered.
And years after Granddad's death,
when his house had to be emptied,

my father and brothers and I worked
for days cataloging all
those books we didn't want sold
for nothing: one would call

out the author, the title,
and the publisher; another would
type it up; and another would put
them in stacks that stood

wall to wall in the library,
the parlor, and the hallway.
Even though my father just sat
and told us what to do that day,

he was there working with us,
helping solve the problem
of what to do with Granddad's library.
Emphysema weakened him

later so that he hardly left his bed,
though he lived long enough
to see the manuals, texts,
medical books, the most valuable stuff

(we'd all thought) sold for almost nothing.
We couldn't even give away
that correspondence school course
in civil engineering.

—∞—

The phone
woke her and she knew
instantly, Mother said. A nurse said he
seemed to be—there is
no word

that suits
what was happening
to him in those early morning hours,
and I don't know what
they said

really—
seemed to be dying
I will say here instead of the going
that first came to mind,
they said

he was
dying—my mother
heard that word singing through the telephone,
and it must have been
the sound

she'd heard
whispered in her dreams.
She got up quickly, dressed, made herself think
of everything,
stepped out

and turned
to lock the door when
she realized it wasn't just dark out
there, there was a fog
so thick

the end
of the lighted porch
was invisible to her. But she kept
going, she walked
on out

toward
the garage, her hand
outstretched, touching nothing, the light behind
her diminished now,
she took

two more
steps, and the planet
dropped away from her, she couldn't even
see her feet. *I am,*
she thought,

going
to the hospital
to be with my husband who is dying.
She took one more step
and closed

her eyes,
and it was the same
darkness either way, eyes closed, eyes open.
She thought it harder
this time:

I am
going. . . . She turned back,
and in four steps she could see the porch light.
She went in and made
coffee

and sat
down at the table
with the empty cup in front of her, she
lost track of time, she
sat there,

and I
was asleep beside
my wife here in Vermont, Charles was asleep
in Rhode Island, Bill
asleep

out west,
all the grandchildren
sleeping, the ninety-seven-year-old mother
in the nursing home
asleep.

But he
was not alone, there
were nurses, Doctor Roda walked up there
to the hospital
knowing

a man
he'd kept alive was
going to—did those people have the right
word, did they say he's
going

to die?
Do I know if they'd
say that? I have to see them there beside
his bed, three of them,
watching

him breathe,
taking his pulse, then
catching each other's eyes when there was no
more breath, no more pulse,
no more

life.
What
words were spoken then,
when they had to turn away from what they
had witnessed? I want
their words

to be
common: *Do you want
some coffee? Is it still foggy out there?*
even *I've got to
take a*

piss. I
want them to be who
they are, my mother in the car later
making her way there
to be

who she
is, my brothers, my
children, my nieces and nephews, even
old deaf grandmama,
I want

no one
ever again like
Mother to have to grope out into that
complete darkness
where it

didn't
matter if she was
alive or dead, for that moment she was
not anywhere and did not
matter.

He was.
I say my father was
here. I say he lived thousands of strong days.
I know he got sick. My
father

died. I
can say that, can walk
from home to work, can touch my daughter's hair,
can say anything
I want.

from *The Nature of Yearning*
(1992)

Local Metaphysics

Finally the mother had to pack up the kids
in the car and take them to see her, Miss
Ossie Price, who had tended Prices' Store
six days a week for the lifetimes of both
generations, though the mother found it hard,
after she'd knocked on the door of the house
and Miss Ossie was standing there, so tired
and still not finished crying but polite
as always, to speak: "Ossie, I'm sorry
to ask this, but the children can't believe you
weren't in the fire. They never saw you
anywhere but in the store. Could you just
come out to the car and let them see you?"
The great burnt corpse that had been Prices' Store
lay just across the street, and it stung her
eyes even to glance that way, but she walked down
there and talked to them through the car window,
three little girls. The youngest, a towhead,
a runny-nosed pretty one named Christine,
sat frozen and wide-eyed until Miss Ossie
opened the door, pulled the child into her
arms, and hugged her close. Finally Christine
cried. Then they thanked Miss Ossie and drove home.
This was in Ivanhoe, Virginia,
a Blue Ridge Mountain town so small there's no
store there at all now that Prices' has burnt.
My mother, who lives there and who heard it
from somebody, told me this, but I've filled
in such details as I need to live with it,
as did my mother and her reliable
source, and as will those children, forgetting
it and holding on to it through the years
until one day that little one, who smelled
to Miss Ossie like a country child in need
of a bath, whose cheek left a smear of tears

and mucus on her dress, will be telling it
to her friend over lunch in some city
restaurant, the story will be spilling
out with such passion that they will both laugh,
and this well-dressed woman with a mountain
twang in her voice will find herself saying,
"This actually happened to me, I
remember it clearly," as in amazement
she asks herself, "Why am I making this up?"

Eastern Standard

Riled by Daylight
Savings, Grandmama
Huddle kept her
clocks unchanged.
Summers she was off
an hour and irked
at the Democrats
responsible
for inflation,
integration,
and now this
further indignity.

Disoriented
her last years
in a nursing home,
she shrank
until she became
an old-lady doll,
restrained in bed
and railing
to the bare,
urine-scented
room about bad food,
bad manners,
and the Kennedys.

At ninety-nine
she finally died.
I'm forty-seven.
Yesterday I stole
an hour
from a clock of hers
that has come down
to me. This morning

when I checked
my watch
against the light
outside the window,
my grandmother
spoke sharply:
"What time
is it, sonny?
And don't you
lie to me!"

STUDY

This morning rain on my skylight
marbles the blue-gray sky and blurs
the maple's branches suffering
the wind from the northeast.
                              A bird
flashes diagonally up
across the wet-streaked glass,
winged shadow there and gone so fast
I barely see it;
                    then standing
at my grandmother's grave, I feel
my mother lean against me, wind
and cold rain slapping our faces
for letting Gran die by herself
in a hateful room;
                        and driving
through mountains in a slick-tired VW
with one headlight gone, I'm swabbing
fog off the windshield while rain turns
to snow;
              dark is coming, and I
am saying good-bye to Linda
Butler on Dundalk Avenue
in thin rain that's chilling us both,
shivering us hard these minutes
that are the last we ever spend
together;
              a boy on a porch
smells rain coming across the fields
and sees his young father running
toward him with drops splattering
his shirt;
              a child out in the yard
hears his aunt laugh as he strips off
clothes in a thunderstorm—

                              quick light
flashing down corridors darkened
by all these years!—
                    as a crow lights,
bobbing a limb of my neighbor's spruce,
or lifts and flies through fifty miles
of rain before it comes to rest.

THE NATURE OF YEARNING

for Lindsey and Bess

I

This northern August swells with warmth
the garden would burst and a trout waits
beneath the moving river surface
he holds steady until the brown caddis
fly floats above him he plunges upward
breaks the silent water then slaps down fat
as deer that graze the flat meadows while slowly
as in a dream of shadows a black bear circles
beneath trees ten thousand shades of green.

II

All changed now quickened the morning
air in September lifts the spirit high
as one perfect trumpet note still
this clarity this concerto suggests
the coming death of tomato vines also
cucumber broccoli corn beans peas yellow
squash cauliflower all vegetables dead
or dying we wait the swelling of pumpkins
the blood flame turning of delicate leaves.

III

High down out of Canada the geese were flying
all day my wife said that far-off honking
sound makes you feel lonely the trees were pure
fire for two weeks but now the leaves have fallen
all purple and brown the woods resound with axes
while men cut logs the children home from school
go out for kindling the leaves crackle the blood
of the animals flows richer and a white tail doe
sniffs the air at dusk her smoky fawn now half grown.

85

IV

Chop the caught turkey's neck catch the buck
deer in gunsights fire shots deep into his heart
sling up his carcass to a thick tree cut open
his belly and handle the bloody heat and stink
of his guts shoot doves partridge quail
pheasant and grouse shoot rabbits shoot quick
squirrels and walk the stubbled fields with meat
on your back for soon the snow comes and with it
the silence at night when the wind wants man flesh.

V

White December the elegance of pine trees
in snow with voices rising in praise of Christ
the soft child of winter all Bach Fasch
and Handel cannot hold Jesus' swelling song
but now the trout takes no food the bass
sinks into the darkest pools of the river
the bear's blood slows while goose and duck
have long flown south and beside the house
snow deepens over logs stacked for the fire.

VI

Ice ice the death of trees the wind strips them bare
it whips them into savage rooted dances branches
crack limbs are yanked off they fall and smatter
on the frozen ground fearing wind I tell my wife
don't stand by that window a pane might burst
this morning she found stiff on the crusty ice
a redpoll dead and light as dust in her hand she said
the sun has forgotten us the nights go on and on
the clouds flee and the wind howls all day long.

VII

No meat in the house we cut holes in the ice
this February we fished for smelt and perch the ice
on the lake was two feet thick my wife thinks
the birds have left us forever only the rats thrive
they steal our corn and leave us just cobs and husks
rabbits are hard to track now but one the other day
sat in the field he was so cold I walked up and kicked
him before I shot the ice builds its kingdom
and holds against what fire we have left love. ,

VIII

We long for warmth these days there is little sun
still no birds have flown north over our house
and I think this March no month for birth only
the wind has life no green anywhere the trees
are just bones they shiver and bend they want
loose from this earth yesterday we saw the grass
it was brown and dead as an old hide in daylight
the snow melts some but it freezes again at night
the ground is covered with brittle crusts of thin ice.

IX

Oh the waters burst there are the timid green buds
delicate grass crocus and daffodil the waters
gather they flow out of the mountain the streams
wash off dead limbs and leaves the gentle rains
bring birth this air of April wakes even the animals
the spring birds have come back the trout leaps again
now the wind is a child the earth is sunlit a woman
walks outside this morning she is beautiful as the clear
sweet sound a man makes with his horn at his lips.

INSIDE THE HUMMINGBIRD AVIARY

Thumb-sized birds in gaudy greens,
iridescent vermilions, stop
on invisible floating dimes
intricately to pivot and kiss

sugar-water bottles or desert
blossoms. Within easy snatching
distance, a Broad-Billed perches,
preens, pisses in a quick squirt,

darts out a tongue half
its body length. Suddenly
suspended at breast level,
a Calliope confronts a man,

marking its possession of that
quadrant of space, the sheer force
of its watch-part heart stopping
the giant, making him laugh.

These wings are the furious
energy of perfect stillness
to make him forget kestrels
and red-masked vultures.

Here in this airy cage
he has seen five whole
hummingbirds fit
into the chambers

of his hog-sized heart.
What the man wants now
is to be desert soil
beneath a thorny bush,

the black tongues of hummers
engineering sweetness
from blossoms that once
were his body.

THE SNOW MONKEY
ARGUES WITH GOD

Four days the mother
snow monkey carries
her stillborn baby
before she leaves it

by a rocky stream. Then
she finds a high place
where she can brood alone
and still see her sisters

with their babies.
For four days she groomed
what should have been
as lively as these others.

If the snow monkey hurts
this way, can she not
also know what death is?
Or at least what it is not:

The thing she left downstream
is not like these babies,
tugging and pulling
at their mothers, trying

to focus four-day-old
eyes on falling water
and sunlight skittering
under moving tree-branches.

While she watches her sisters
tenderly nursing
their young, she must feel
the wordless

old quarrel: better
that this paradise be burnt
to a clean white ash
than for any living

creature to have to lay down
on streamside rocks
what has been loved, what
stinks to high heaven.

LOVE AND ART

At the Chagall exhibit
the woman moves slowly
from picture to picture.

The man hardly pauses.
He eats the pictures,
wishing he could have
them all for himself.

Bella with a White Collar
surrounds the woman, as God
must cradle the universe.

The man strides past *The Wedding,
Bride and Groom of the Eiffel Tower,*
all of *Daphnis and Chloe.*
He is eager to buy postcards.

At the *Magic Flute* costumes,
the woman suddenly hears Chagall
and Mozart telling jokes, filling
the museum with their laughter.

The man buys a *Fall of Icarus*
T-shirt and a *Milking the Cow* poster
for the kids and sits down to wait.

Bella Writing is where she stops,
knowing the moment the painter
found her like that and took up
what was handy, a page of notepaper,

and that is where he finds her,
standing with strangers, brushing
her eyes, and smiling into the light.

Upstairs Hallway, 5 a.m.

My daughter's voice
wafts into the dark
through which, freshly
showered and shaved,
I am feeling my way.
I stop and listen
but hear only the house
hum, click, and groan.

A friend says a voice
on the phone instantly
reveals sex, age, ethnic
background, education,
and intelligence.

But from this sentence
spoken out of her
dreams by my child,
I discern no words,
only a tone: quiet,
serious, friendly,
somewhat formal.

The dead must hear
their living speak
just this way: *Yes,*
you are there forever
running your fingers
along the cool wall
of darkness, while I
so deeply dream this
world of sunlit shapes.
Soon enough I shall be
moving behind you.
Please, let me sleep
a little longer.

CLOSE

for Ted Littwin and Lyn Mattoon

My friend tells me how,
in his childhood, his father
rose early, then got lonely
and so came to stand
over my friend's bed.

My friend says he would wake
from a deep sleep, aware
of his father's presence,
would sit straight up in bed
and say, "What are you doing in here?"

"Oh nothing," his father
would reply. "I wasn't bothering
anything, but now that you're up . . ."
and then they would be talking
all through those impossible hours.

Later, drinking and talking,
my friend and I consider the coming
death of the planet. "It's no longer
a matter of pushing a button
we don't want to push," I say.

He says, "Yes, all we have to do
is live exactly as we're living
right now." And I murmur,
"What do you think we have,
maybe a hundred years?"

Nodding with understanding how
we mean to murder our children,
he and I pierce our loneliness.
My own father is dead and anyway never
stood by my bed in the dark.

Catch

Barehanded, my father
caught my first throws.

Later I saw him
wincing but thought

his pain small
compared to my need

for dignity
at recess.

When he thought
I was old enough,

he began to fire
fast balls that stung

my fingers, that one
May dusk made me

cry and walk
into the house.

Ashamed in my room,
I heard him explain

what was wrong
to Mother downstairs.

Now when Molly asks
me to play catch

and she's got our
house's one glove,

my father softly
sighs, All right, son.

In my bare palm
I feel him

feeling what
I thought

I had
to give him.

THINKING ABOUT MY FATHER

I have to go back
past the way he was
at the end, panting
for breath, begging
for medicine, crazy
from medicine taken
for years. This is
hard because in his
dying, he was vivid,
excruciatingly slow,
and profoundly self-
absorbed, as if his
death required more
energy and devotion
than we could ever
bring to his bedside.

But then there he is
at home, at his desk
in the den, where he
was able to be most
truly himself, paying
bills—he was happy
doing that—reading
the paper, then best
of all, beautifully
solving its crossword
puzzle. My father was
the absolute master
of crossword puzzles
in the *Roanoke Times*.

I do not mean to say
that he shut himself
off from us. It was

just that we learned
to approach his desk
for quiet attention.
He breathed a light
whistle between his
teeth while he helped
me balance my paper
route money, coat my
model airplane's silk
wing with banana oil,
hinge a new Brazilian
stamp into my album.

My father did things
with a care that was
more important to him
than the thing itself.
For example, painting
by the numbers: no one
ever number-painted so
gravely and precisely.
His Saint Bernards hang
over his desk, his blue
jays over the toilet so
that every peeing male
must witness the craft
of his terrible picture.

His pleasures were fresh
things, mail just pulled
from his post office box,
unthumbed newspapers, new
model-airplane kits, sets
of mint-condition stamps
in glassine envelopes.
With his hands he savored
a new harmonica so that I
still see as sacred those

little Hohner boxes with
pictures on them of old-
time German concert bands.

I don't have any fresh
insight into my father
or his life. Thinking
about him like this, I
miss him, and I forget
how horrible his death
was. Some mornings I
wake up feeling bad for
no reason I can think of,
and then all day he'll be
on my mind, dying again.

I have no memory of his
holding me as an infant,
but we have an old home
movie in which my twenty-
two-year-old mother walks
out onto the front porch
and hands a baby to this
thin young man. Some days
I wake up limp and happy
as that child, smiled at
and lifted up to the sun
by someone who wanted me
right here in this world.

Summer Lake

The slow coming of dusk over the water
enthralls the husband and wife.
What soft shades of light the lake
and sky turn, such dark lavenders
and pinks they must believe their wish
to be happy together has produced this
world around them.
                    Here on the rocky
beach at the back of the park
an old man playing an accordion
turns toward them, cocks his head,
and launches a serenade. A blue van
he has apparently driven here
holds a woman and some children
who sit inside it, unmoving, staring
out over the water.
                    The aching husband
puts his arm around his soul-tired
wife's shoulders, she puts hers
around his waist, and they stand like that
on the grassy slope above the beach
listening,
          because the old musician
seems accomplished, squeezing and pulling
a stream of notes from the instrument
rippling his fingers up and down
its buttons and keys, smiling at them
as he plays.
             "He's brilliant, or else
he's terrible," the wife murmurs
in that way they've come to speak, out
toward some disinterested witness,
but her husband is in a mood to take it
intimately and so nods and says, "Yes,

I've never heard anything like that. Maybe
it's wonderful."
                    But they don't know
what to make of the music, though they try
to listen even harder. The notes sound
crushed together, too many and too strange.
"I don't like it," the wife finally says,
abruptly turning away and walking across the grass
with her head down.
                    Silky light
gilds the water, the accordion man grins,
and the park's spring green burns
his eyes, so that the husband must turn
to catch up with his wife in her pale dress
steadily moving into the shadow
of houses, trees, gardens, and lawns.
                              Later,
riding the ferry across the lake, he
and she stand at the rear of the boat,
gazing back across the wake's churned-up
froth and long ripples of inky blue water
toward the lakeside park, where now
there is no battered blue van, nothing
but a light rim of beach stones beneath
the deep green of grass and trees almost
in darkness.
                    Why they stand back here,
instead of forward with the other passengers
taking the wind in their faces and smiling
toward the lighted city is not something
these two wish to discuss. But they know this
is what they want: to study the receding
shore haloed by dull pink light, stand
together without touching, and go on
hearing what the little man played for them.

from *A David Huddle Reader*
(1994)

Mother Encounters Monkey at the Post Office

And because I have written so much about Monkey,
she brings him home with her to talk with me.

I don't like to talk at eight thirty in the morning,
I write on my laptop computer until well after nine.

It was as a boy that I had so much to say to Monkey,
who is eighty-two years old and *Deaf now*, he shouts

at me, *Can't hear a thing, honey, but that's how*
the Lord meant things to be, I guess. We don't always

understand, now do we, honey? You know about Jonah
and the whale, don't you? I know you do. I went to school

with your mother, did you know that? First I went
to school with your daddy, then I went to school

with your mother; they went on ahead, and I stayed
right there till they told me I could quit,

and then I went to work for your granddaddy. I guess
you remember that time Charles fell off the threshing

machine and I caught him? Well, the Bible tells us
we can't always understand. I've still got my health,

and I've still got my Bible—Monkey pats his overalls
chest pocket. His simian eyes take on this abstracted

look as if an inner voice is giving him instructions,
to which he must listen carefully before deciding

what to do next. I hear stirring upstairs that means
Lindsey, Bess, and Molly have wakened to Monkey's and my

conversation. You're looking good, Monkey, I tell him
quietly. You look just like you did forty years ago.

Monkey doesn't hear my fatuous remarks. He smiles and rises.
Well, I better be getting down the hill, he says,

and when I offer him a ride, he sweetly refuses. *Next time
you come home for a visit, I hope I'll see you. We're all*

real proud of you, he says. When I was a boy,
he never did this, but he does now, gives me a good-bye hug,

which I stiffly try my best to return. Then Monkey walks
down through the field of high wet grass toward Ivanhoe, leaving

my mother and me to explain to each other, and a little later
to Lindsey and Bess and Molly, when they come downstairs

looking quizzical, what has transpired that required
such a lot of shouting in the living room this morning.

WHY I LIKE OPERA

for James Alan McPherson

These sweet voices
of *Le Nozze Di Figaro*
shaping elegant passion
from my living-room speakers
please me while I type
on my laptop computer.

In Ivanhoe, Virginia,
where I grew up,
I desired music
from the radio of a passing car:
I got a hot-rod Ford / and a two-dollar bill,
and I know a spot / just over the hill,

and Pete Bushey, my fourth-grade classmate
now serving life in prison,
in a certain mood,
might have murdered someone
who asked to hear Mozart.

The boy who survived
that childhood would not recognize
the man he became.

So do I long for those old days?

Like that late Sunday afternoon
in front of the Pentecostal Holiness Church,
when Leon Jones tried
to slice open my belly
with his pocket knife?

Qui mormora il ruscel, qui scherza l'aura,
che col dolce susurro il cor ristaura.
Qui ridono i fioretti é l'erba è fresca, *
as when I was growing up
no one ever dreamed
of saying.

*Here murmurs the stream, here sports the breeze,
  Which refreshes the heart with its sweet whispers,
  Here flowers smile and the grass is cool.

What You Live For

Men's Sauna

Boy about seven's hanging
around outside the sauna.
Naked, pale, thin-chested,
he steps back, startled,

when I reach for the door,
looks up at me with ostrich
eyes, glasses that magnify
so much he must be almost

legally blind. What's funny
is just before I step in,
I notice the kid's pencil
stub of a pecker, such a joke

I almost want to say, *Hey,
kid, don't worry, it'll grow.*
Inside, there's a beefy guy,
sweaty slab of meat reading

a newspaper. I don't know
what it is about the sauna,
the heat, I guess, or being
naked in that coop of a room,

but I get a little hostile
when I'm in there. Somebody
once told me he'd never met
anybody from Texas who wasn't

an asshole. I never shared
a sauna with anybody I didn't
suspect was an asshole, too,
and I know this doesn't shine

the brightest light on me, but
anyway, right off, I don't
like this guy, don't like
his pink skin, his moustache,

his posture, or even the way
his prick and balls hang,
which of course has nothing
to do with what kind of human

being the man is, and I'm used
to such sentiments arising
in me when I'm in the sauna,
I can stand it in there only

about ten minutes anyway, so no
big deal, this Texan and I
settle into sweating in silence,
when the door opens, and the boy

outside holds it open while he
addresses my sauna partner,
who must be the father.
The boy's voice is too low

for me to hear what he says,
and the angle of the room
keeps me from seeing the kid,
so the data I get is his dad,

who says, "Tie your sneakers
for me, will you? Why don't you go
on upstairs and find your mom?
Find your mom, will you?"

The guy speaks over his newspaper
and doesn't move, the door stays
open while the boy murmurs something
else, the cool air streaming in

all the while. I expect the guy
to say, *Shut the door, will you?*
but he doesn't, he just repeats,
"Go upstairs and find your mom."

The door does finally close,
and the boy's dad and I are alone
again, naked, silent, and sitting
three feet away from each other.

I have this urge to say,
*Did you know that your voice
makes it evident that you hate
your kid? And if I can hear it,*

*you know for sure that your kid
hears it, too.* I don't say that,
of course, though the sauna
makes me nearly crazy enough

to say it, but I have in mind
this cautionary tale a friend
told me about getting the shit
beat out of him in a Jacuzzi

by some guys he'd insulted—
he said it was pretty mythic.
Naked, he got pounded bloody,
and they almost drowned him.

I'm way past the age of wanting
to fight, even though hostility
still has its little condo
in my emotional village.

Also, I'm a father of daughters,
girls who often enough give me
looks that say, *My God, is that
how it is with you men? You're*

all crazy! I know they study
me, their model male, the one
by which they'll measure all
other men who approach them.

So I stay quiet enough to hear
my sweat drops hit the bench slats
and the boy's dad's breathing.
What I don't hear but feel anyway

is how this guy's ashamed
of his boy, this guy wishes
his kid were bigger, louder,
had a prick that didn't make

him want to laugh out loud,
and for Christ's sake didn't
have to wear those stupid bug-eye
glasses. That's what I hate,

when my good buzz of hostility
turns into this pissy pity.
I'm down off the bench and out
the door and into the shower,

taking the water as cold
as I can stand it. But here's
what's weird here, the guy
just keeps staying in there.

I'm out of the shower,
toweled dry, dressed, and combing
my hair, when it occurs to me
that he's got to have been

in there half an hour by now,
which to me would be torture,
assuming I could even force
myself to stay in there so long.

I've got my gym bag packed up
and my coat on when the boy,
dressed now in a hockey jersey
that makes me notice how thin

his shoulders are, trudges by me
on his way back to the sauna door
to have another word with his dad.
I don't hear it. I'm out of there.

Military Parachuting Exercise

The ninth of the nine jump commands is *jump*.
Once you do that—and if you're too scared

to push yourself out, why, they shove you out
anyway—you experience a moment

(the soul's release from the body at death!)
when the plane moves away and you're just

suspended in silence so immaculate
that the angel who has slept within you

suddenly wakes and out of your chest rips
this heavenly cry—aaaaahhhh!—which means *God,*

I'm flying toward You. That feeling ends
in an instant—it was mere delusion.

At first you didn't feel the fall, but now
gravity's pulling you down, whereas surely

the soul soars upward in its joyful flight
toward paradise. Nevertheless, floating

at twelve hundred feet, you enter stillness
that seems enormous, not the dead quiet

of outer space, but a living absence
of sound, as if great chords will soon resound,

thunderous sentences will fill the air.
Silence like that—not to mention the sweep

of space and landscape—makes mere soldiers both
anxious and bored, and so one calls out

to another fifty yards down and away
(the plane leaves jumpers in a stair-stepped line),

Hey, man, he'll say, *what's the weather like
down there?* and however banal his words,

however puny his voice, the pure air
carries the noise, so that the soldiers

begin talking as they fall toward earth.
I almost shit my pants! shouts one. Another

replies, *Whaddaya mean almost?* You laugh.
The nearer the ground the faster you seem

to fall, and so fear shuts you up. The field
begins rushing at you. If you look straight

down, you'll curl your legs up. It's human
to flinch like that. Here's what you have to do:

stare at the horizon, relax your body,
when you feel your toes brushing the ground, just

twist and roll in whatever direction
you're already moving, give your body

to physics and matter. A somersault
comes naturally—and so does chasing

down your chute. You've got to catch that thing
and collapse it, or else the wind can catch it,

it'll drag you across some farmer's field,
and turn you into a bloody piece of meat.

Two-Joke Man

Big guy,
stays in his studio all day and half the night,
see him
at dinner, that's the only time.
Writer,
but I don't know his books, he doesn't know mine,
at least
that was my impression the one time we talked.
Jerry.

Badanes is his last name, B-A-D-A-N-E-S,
eighteen
different ways to pronounce a name like that,
Spanish,
Greek, and so on—Jewish is actually what he was—
his one
published book's on the holocaust, book
he worked
on half a lifetime, because this guy's in his fifties,
like me.

So anyway,
you don't see Jerry all day, and then you see him
at dinner.
And the man becomes very visible at dinner, very audible—
a presence
is what he is among us big-ego artist types,
but he's sweet,
you know, which is rare, most of us are anything but that.
And Jerry
likes to talk, likes to tell us stories, most of all likes
to tell us
jokes, except that so far as I can tell from my brief acquaintance
with the man, two is all he's got. He's a
two-joke man.

Here's one:
Postman delivering the mail, finds the lady of the house standing
inside the screen door, wearing a see-through negligee. "Come in,"
she says. "I've made lunch for you."
Postman
goes in, sits down at the table with her, the two of them eat this
lovely lunch she's fixed. Postman uses his napkin and says, "Thank you
this has been great, but I've got to finish delivering
the mail."
Lady of the house stands up and says,

"Come upstairs,
I've got something for you." Postman follows her up, they make love
in her bedroom, wild, crazy love like you read about, until finally
the postman, exhausted and happy,
says, "Thank you,
this has been great, but I really do have to finish delivering
the mail," and he begins getting dressed. Lady climbs out of bed,
goes to her purse on the dresser, takes out a dollar, hands it to him.
Postman stands there staring at the dollar bill. "What the hell
is this?" he says. "I come here to deliver your mail,

you fix me
lunch, you take me up here, we make love all afternoon, now you give me
this dollar. I mean, what the hell is this?" Lady of the house
tells him, "Look, this morning I ask my husband,

what should I
give the postman for Christmas? My husband says,
'Fuck him,
give him a dollar.' The lunch was my idea."

So that's one
joke Jerry tells—I hear him tell that once twice or maybe
three times,
I don't know. The other one is the penguin joke. Here's
how it goes:
Traffic cop at a busy intersection in New York is going
crazy
directing traffic, blowing his whistle, pointing, gesturing,
stopping cars,
shouting, furiously waving, and so on when he sees
this car

full of penguins, and they're bouncing around in there
every
which way, just bouncing up and down the way penguins do,
and the cop
gets really mad. He blows his whistle and raises
his hand
to stop the car, and he walks over to the driver's side
and leans
into the window and says, "What the hell do you think
you're doing
with this car full of penguins? I want you to take
these penguins
straight to the zoo. Do you hear me? I want you to take
these penguins
to the zoo!" Driver says, "Yes sir. Yes sir," drives
on through
the intersection, and the cop feels fine now, he's done
something
worthwhile. Next day, he's out there again, same spot,
same crazy
traffic, he's whistling and pointing and waving, when what

does he see
but the same car full of penguins, and they're bouncing
all around
in there, except this time, they're bouncing in unison like,
and they've got
these baseball caps on. The cop is just furious.
He blows
his whistle, stops all traffic, stops the penguin car,
walks over
and says to the driver, "What the hell do you think
you're doing?
Didn't I tell you to take these penguins
to the zoo?"
Driver nods and says, "Yes sir. I did. We went to the zoo. We had
a wonderful time. Today we thought we'd go to a ball game."

So that's it.
That's Jerry and his two jokes, and the sad part of this
whole thing
is that Jerry died last fall, heart attack, no surprise,
overweight,
no exercise, never did anything but work on his manuscript
and talk
to people at dinner. And of course I wish
I'd known him
better, been around him more, read his book, been his pal
and so on,
the usual wishy-washy remorseful sentiments.
One thing more
to tell you, then I'll shut up. There was this woman,
this young
composer there from New York, so totally from New York
you wonder
she could survive anywhere else, and she always sat at
Jerry's table
at dinner, and if Jerry didn't find a way to tell the penguin
joke on his own, why then she would request it. "Tell about the
penguins,"

she would say, and Jerry would glance at her with this sly
expression,
and he would say, "You want me to tell that one, huh?"
and he would,
he would tell it again, tell it just as well as he had the last time,
and the time before that, and she would
always laugh
and look at him and shake her head and blush with pleasure,
and Jerry,
he'd modestly examine his silverware or something,
but grin
nevertheless, and there'd be this little moment
of quiet
at the table before she'd say, "That's nice, Jerry. That's just
so nice."

Two

1

In our neighborhood a Chinese woman
marches our sidewalks with a face
that says, I hate this place,
I hate you, I hate all your kind.

Other days I see her with the woman
who must be her daughter. These two
walk arm in arm, speaking closely,
smiling as if they're home

in their mountain village, it's springtime,
and the last war ended years ago.
How can I know what they tell each other?
How can I hear the older woman when she says,

My darling one, please forgive him,
you know tomorrow he'll be contrite.
He'll buy you another yellow bowl
and carry it to you filled with blossoms.

Again it is the older woman who speaks,
Now why must you go away so soon? Can you not
stay longer with me? Only you understand me.
Come, walk closer with me! I want to sing with you.

Then as these two walk, they begin singing
so softly I can't possibly hear them,
and they don't even use a language I know:
Moving puzzle of light, goes their song,

shadows the willow makes on this earth—
can the leaves ever know the wind again
if you do not turn your face to me,
if you do not return my smile?

2

Among moving cars stands a retriever,
wagging its tail—in four lanes
of stopping, starting drivers.
These cars aren't sheep, the dog says

nervously. It's not so much afraid
as uncertain. It moves—it's almost
hit!—then again. This is too hard to watch,
but stopped here, we can't help it. *What to do?*

In one lane, a truck's stopped with the driver
leaning out its window, the dog staring up
at him—*Please tell me what to do,*
says the dog, certain the man knows

and will tell him any moment now, *Come? Sit?
Stay? Go get the bird? Please, sir, what
do you want of me?* We wonder, too, what
command will make sense of this, what

can possibly explain it—busy intersection,
man in the truck, golden retriever in the street.
Did the dog anger the master? Are drugs
to blame? Divorce? *I know you're not trying*

to abandon me. The dog calmly pants. *I know
you wouldn't do that.* Finally the man
pulls across traffic into a service station,
the dog trotting behind the truck. That's when

our light changes. That's when
we leave them, the dog still wagging
its tail, gazing up at the driver
who's still leaning out his truck window.

My wife says, "That didn't make sense."
We're driving south on Route 7,
which, at the moment, makes sublime sense
to us. We don't know exactly what that was

we saw back there, we just know
we're not there yet,
the place where what you live for
just about kills you.

Confessions

1

I try to be an artist
so that I don't have to be a complete
whore;
        therefore, priests
of all varieties
interest me. Distantly
I've admired some.
                    I saw one,
a Father James Newsome,
whom I served as an acolyte
for the eight o'clock Communion Service
at St. John's Episcopal Church
in Wytheville, Virginia, one Sunday in 1958,
pop a sweat
as he was speaking from the Book of Prayer
and moving his hands
over the chalice.
               It gave me the chills
because I was standing close enough to touch his robes,
and I could hear the belief
when it came into his voice.
                    I think
it must be like that
for the good priests,
God coming into you,
God going back out, like a quick
shot of electrical current,
then you have to wait and hope
it happens again.
             Anyway
that's my ultimate religious experience.

The whole
fifty-two seconds it was happening,
what I was most aware of
was it was
Father Newsome's faith,
it was his,
not mine.

2

To pray,
my grandfather's hired man,
Monkey Dunford,
an illiterate, unsanitary,
deeply ignorant
and deeply kind
Holy Roller
at lunch (or dinner as they called it)
set himself apart
from the other men
and my grandfather and me.
Monkey went to the barn,
where he knelt among the hay bales,
and shouted his prayers
loudly enough to be heard by us
sitting around the toolshop.
Monkey's prayers
sounding in the distance
made the men snicker
or sneer or just shake their heads.
Monkey sometimes prayed
thirty minutes or more.
                         As a boy
I traipsed along with Monkey
while he did his chores—
feeding and milking the cows,
shoveling out the stalls,
weeding the garden, sweeping the kitchen,

and sometimes even cooking
my grandmother's breakfast
and cleaning up after her.
Monkey and I talked at length
about many topics, including God
and Christ and praying.
                              I condescended
to Monkey, I know that, and I still do
when I think or write about him.
The years are falling away now,
and I'm still studying him—
still seeing his home-scissored hair,
his glittering, too-far-apart eyes
and leathery skin, his lifted brows
and wrinkled forehead, as he regarded me,
waiting for me to say or do
                              I don't know what.
I even sometimes still get whiffs
of that dirt-and-sweat, piss-and-shit fragrance
of Monkey.
                    It's coming to me,
                                   how he was
my teacher, and how until I die
I'll be his
disciple.

The Fall as I Have Known It

Most intensely longed for when I was a boy
was a palomino like Trigger, with of course
a silver-trimmed saddle, matching holsters
and six-guns. . . . First on my list, that horse
wasn't something I wanted by itself,
it was just essential to my cowboy
ensemble. After all, my grandfather
had work horses that had no use for boys
like me. I also wanted a panther,
preferably in black, like the Tarzan
comics—not the films—or even better,
like Kipling's wise Bagheera, a creature
willing to counsel and offer advice
in tough situations, not to mention
being so scary nobody'd ever
pick on a boy with a pet like that.

As an adult I've gone through my birds phase:
I watched them, I fed them, I even kept
a record of which ones I saw that winter
and spring I lived in a cabin and wrote.
Here at home I hung a bird feeder near
the living-room window and watched sparrows,
jays, finches, and chickadees fight for the seeds
the squirrels didn't get. That spring, I hosed
from underneath the feeder a layer
of bird shit a quarter of an inch thick.
I still like birds, but feeding them is no
longer how I wish to relate to them.
I like to think about their bones and how
their intelligence is dispersed throughout
their bodies—brain no more significant
than tail-feather, beak, wing, craw, or talon.
I even like trying to imagine
the natural death of a bird. I want
it to be possible for one to die

129

mid-flight. Birds don't have souls, I'm sure of that.
That's the whole point of a bird, not
to be weighed down with something that heavy.
It's okay to hate crows, too, I think.
That's the whole point of a crow. They get
frustrated when we don't hate them enough.

It's my mother coming up in me when
I start going on like that, one silly
notion after another. A program
on hawks and owls captured my attention
last night. A goshawk hanging in the air
with its legs relaxed looks vulnerable,
like a child picked up or a man falling.
An owl's round face as it flies seems as sweet
as the man-in-the-moon's. But birds correct
my sentiments. A hawk snares a pheasant
mid-flight—my wish come true!—then on the ground
gouges out gobbets before the pheasant
has even finished dying. All right! Amen!
My mother never said so, but I think
she liked it, too, how Mother Nature is
actually the meanest motherfucker
in the valley. Well, anyway, a horse
—even a trained and groomed palomino—
is not what I want anymore. Neither
is a panther. A nice goshawk maybe.
Just kidding. The truth is Henry and I
want a puppy. Henry's our chocolate
Labrador retriever, three years old now,
neutered and so well trained he won't even
shed a hair unless we give the command,
"Shed, Henry! Shed!" A dog of the nineties,
Henry needs a puppy to compensate
for the planetary anxiety
that floats freely throughout his consciousness.
Me, too, I'd like a puppy, and I'd prefer
it either in chocolate to match Henry,
or else in white, which would contrast nicely.

THE UNCLES

1

Uncle Bill once drove east with light-green globes
of wine in the trunk of his Oldsmobile.
When he and Aunt Irene told about California,
my brothers and I noticed how our parents listened

as if, if they could, they would leave us
and our house in Virginia and move out west
where it was always sunny, where they actually grew
the grapes for that wine they were sipping.

Uncle Bill told us about gold mines in Cyprus
and riding a train all the way across Russia.
Some Russians didn't love Americans, he said,
and so he told them his name was Huddliskovich.

When Uncle Bill laughed, we knew it was because
he had a thousand secrets he would never tell.
To us boys, Uncle Bill was like Lowell Thomas:
what he said was the truth of the world.

2

Uncle Jack from Rome, Georgia,
Uncle Jack the Rambling Wreck
from Georgia Tech, football player,
lawyer, soldier, Major Jack Kent,

United States Army Infantry,
whose ribboned chest bears
two Purple Hearts and a Silver Star,
whose wire-rimmed glasses shine

and whose smile is so American
it hurts to look at his picture—
this man once came to visit us,
took me out into the side yard,

and threw me several perfectly
spiraled passes before he got short
of breath and had to go back inside
for a drink and another cigarette.

3

Every spring Uncle
Will Washington
brought his mule
to plow our garden.

"Why do we call him Uncle?"
Mother looked perplexed.
"I don't know," she said.
"It's just what we do."

4

Uncle C.B. from Princeton, West Virginia,
who ran the store for a coal mining company,
one family reunion brought my brothers and me
—new in their boxes—Mickey Mouse watches.

All that day I couldn't stop
looking at mine on my wrist.
The aunts who kept asking me what time it was
laughed when I told them.

All my life I believed
the reason my Aunt Stella
was so crippled she could hardly walk
was that she had polio as a child.

When I was fifty-two I found out
when she was a baby,
there was an accident with a stroller.
Her older brother was responsible.

To help the children—C.B. and Stella—
live with it,
the family made it up
about the polio.

5

In a tree
in a Fellini movie,
forlornly calling out,
"I—want—a—woman!

I—want—
a—woman!"
sits the uncle
I cherish.

Picture

Early each morning of his later life,
my grandfather walked from his house
up a hill through his untended orchard

to his shop filled with tools
and machines, to the dark room
in back—his office—where his desk

waited beneath a hanging lightbulb.
Here he sat most of every day,
smoking, talking with the men

who worked for him or the men
who came up there to visit a man
who had such a place for himself,

a dim room cluttered with papers
and magazines, with delicate scales,
bottles and jars of chemicals,

shelves of books, a cooler for beer,
and even a palm-sized metal statue
of a squatting dog into whose butt

could be inserted a pellet
that when lit generated a turd
of astonishing length. As a boy,

I studied my grandfather,
that intricate man
who piled the details

of his life around himself
as, when younger, I surrounded myself
with toys in my sandbox.

He was short, bald,
plump, and homely.
Except for Christmas

and trips to Wytheville,
he wore a khaki shirt,
khaki pants, and a khaki hat.

Each day he shaved and smoked
a pack of Camel cigarettes; on Saturdays
he took a bath. My grandfather

owned a farm with hundreds of animals.
He owned buildings, machines, tools,
books, vehicles, lumber, art supplies,

fishing and photography equipment.
If I asked him a question,
my grandfather gave me an answer.

He almost never said, "I don't know,"
because he usually did know
at least something about anything

a boy could think to ask him. His life
was there for me to see—for anyone
to see, really, but he knew I was the one

most interested—and not just in the parts
but in all of it, in everything
that was him. My grandfather let me witness

who he was. Of course he died
years ago. All his things
have been dispersed or sold.

His house (that place he walked away from
each morning) caught fire and burnt
to the ground. Often he let me light

that pellet that made a dog turd,
that made his men laugh and spit.
Once he even let me turn

his beer bottle up to my mouth
for a gulp I choked out my nose.
My grandfather let me know

how he hated my grandmother
fuming at the cook down at the house,
my grandmother angry at the nation

that would take away her servants,
would say she should hold a job,
and require her to help pay for the poor.

I am the boy who understood the man
who every day walked away from her and out
of his house to sit in a dark room

where she wouldn't follow him. She couldn't
see him there, doing nothing but smoking
for hours at a time. On his desk was a thing

that, when I was eleven, he let me study
as long as I wished, a glass paperweight
with a black-and-white (but mostly gray)

picture of a woman, standing, her head
bowed into shadow but her nude body
facing the camera and leaning

forward as if she were the model
for that Greek statue with missing arms.
"What you looking at, boy?"

one of his men asked once, startling me
into open-mouthed silence. I'd never
had to explain it to my grandfather.

It wasn't just her breasts or the dark
shadow of her pubis or even the whole
shape of her that seemed to answer

a question my mind always proposed.
It was how she turned into herself,
held herself back—even though naked

to the camera—from me, from my grandfather
and his men, from all of us everywhere.
"Leave him alone," my grandfather said,

winking at the man and then at me.
"That boy's just doing his homework."
His men got quiet and listened

to the old man. "He's gonna need to know
everything he's learning right now."

MODEL FATHER

Now when I say my father
—meaning his smell of carbide
and cigarettes, his curtain
of opened and held-up
newspaper, the red dents
at either side of the bridge
of his nose, the parchment skin
on the backs of his hands,
and his thick thumb that to me
meant he was a grown man
and that has in recent years
attached itself to my hand—

I'm really saying my father isn't
in my life anymore, except
in just this way—when I choose
words to assemble him,
as when he and I sometimes chose
to spend a Saturday afternoon
at a newspaper-covered card table
gluing together small pieces
of balsa, keeping quiet
company without much regard
for whether or not what
we made would fly.

Ooly Pop a Cow

for Bess and Molly

My brother Charles
brought home the news
the kids were saying
take a flying leap
and eat me raw
and be bop a lula.

Forty miles he rode
the bus there and back.
The dog and I met him
at the door, panting
for hoke poke, hoke
de waddy waddy hoke poke.

In Cu Chi, Vietnam,
I heard tapes somebody's
sister sent of wild thing,
I think I love you
and hey now, what's that
sound, everybody look what's . . .

Now it's my daughters
bringing home no-duh,
rock out, whatever,
like I totally
paused, and like
I'm like . . .

I'm like Mother, her hands
in biscuit dough,
her ears turning red
from ain' nothin butta,
blue monday, and
tutti fruiti, aw rooty!

Dogs & My Mother

An almost collie lies
adoringly beside her
in the picture
of her at thirteen.

Country strays
presented themselves.
When she needed a dog,
she fed one, and it stayed.

While she raised her sons,
Missy and Daisy, Butch
and Pal, each took
its place beside her.

We boys moved away.
My father died.
Barkley, Red, and Lionel
came and stayed awhile.

One morning one didn't
show up. That missing
one had her mourning until
the next came around.

One got shot by boys
showing off, another
got rabies, and that one
she had to shoot herself.

When Shep tried to bite
my wife, he had to be
driven to the vet's
to be put down.

All these dogs
are emblems of sadness—
mine or hers,
I don't know.

Hundreds of mornings
they waited
for her
to come downstairs,

to let them in,
to feed them,
to talk to them
while she built the fire.

Each came in its turn—
Brownie who ate Kleenex,
Lady who took walks with her,
Big Boy the fat M&M eater,

and Robert the rakish
bandit she called
for longest
when he disappeared.

My mother is in a home
in Georgia now.
I'm the one with a dog
in the house.

Basket

Needlepoint for the church
she did back when she could, a strip
of kneeler-facing she pretended
to do after she couldn't anymore:

now she's never out of her room
without the basket of it,
fussing at recreation hour,
teasing out the same old limp piece,

clucking and shaking her head at it.
It's in her lap when they sit,
as they do after meals,
out by the station,

Mrs. Webb, Althea Fromberg, Ella
What'shername, and the others,
the dreadful others
my mother despises.

But who, anyway, can work
in such light?—
this unnatural buzzing
glare that makes these old

fools moan, drool, fall napping
into their trays. . . . My mother
rises and begins to walk away.
The light chases her

down corridors . . . all
the same, this is so . . .
and where's her . . . basket?
Someone has taken it

again, goddamn it,
she hates . . . just wants
to . . .
            When they
hear her crying and come

to the corner where she
has crumpled to the floor,
the aides know what is wrong,
they know what to do.

"Has anybody seen
Mrs. Huddle's basket?"
they call out to the ladies
by the station, because

they all know this part.
"Here it is!" Althea pipes up.
Another calls out, "Here—
she left it here." One lifts it

with two hands into the light
and gives it over. The aides carry it
to her, my mother on the floor,
who grabs and clutches

the thing to her chest. She cries
a little more, getting up,
letting them guide her
back to her room, her bed.

They set the basket
on the blanket right
beside her—"See, now here
it is, Mrs. Huddle."

At last my mother can sleep.
Under its lid and mere
inches from her hand,
her coiled cobra can rest, too.

THE EPISODES

1

On the phone the sheriff explained
she'd called and told them to come
right away, her boys were missing.
They found her in the yard, calling

—calling so hard she was hoarse now—
for my brother and me, who had been
playing out here. We were seven
and five. She couldn't reach my father

at the carbide plant. "Please find
my little boys," she wailed,
so distraught the deputies wanted
to believe her—except they could see

she was too old to be a young
mother, they knew the carbide plant
had closed down years ago, and when
they asked her what year it was,

she looked at them like they were
the biggest fools she'd ever seen.
Voice about to break, she asked them,
"Officers, what year do you think it is?"

2

On the phone Sammy Crockett explained
it wasn't any of his business, he knew that,
but for years our families had been friends,
and he'd seen my mother in town that day.

She looked like she'd just gotten out of bed.
Were we sure that colored woman
we'd gotten to look after her
was doing the job?

3

The history the checkbook tells
told she wrote checks to every mail
and phone solicitation, she wrote
generous checks to Catherine

and to the boy who brought in her coal
and wood, generous checks to her children
and grandchildren—that was us. It was her
money, of course. Then it became garbled,

checks weren't entered, checks
came back unsigned, bills were not paid
or paid twice or three times, the math
was chaos. My brother tried driving

up there from Georgia once a month to pay
the bills and keep the books straight,
but she wrote checks more and more wildly,
a rash of one and two hundred dollar ones

made out to cash, and when he asked her
what those were for, she said—a little slyly,
he thought—"Well, you know, son, it takes
a lot of money to run this house."

4

When he had to take her car away from her
—actually had to drive it away from the house,
because she had hidden extra sets of keys—
she wept and cursed, she said our father

would be ashamed of him for treating her
this way, she said he wouldn't treat a dog
like this. My brother, a retired colonel,
a fighter pilot who flew two tours

in Vietnam and daily combat missions
in Operation Desert Storm, wept that night
in the motel with his wife. He said
it was the worst experience of his life.

5

I don't really want to tell this,
but I know I have to. One rainy night
she walked out of the house and down
through the fields—this was how,

when she was a girl, she walked to school,
except now the paths have grown up in cedars
and broom sage and briars, but anyway—
she made her way to the front porch

of one Philip Campbell, a young man
whose father had worked at the plant
for my father. My mother
presented herself to Mr. Campbell,

soaking wet, her arms scratched up,
her hair wild, her clothes muddy and ripped.
I don't know what she said.
I don't know what he said.

On the phone my brother's wife explained
something that came from Catherine,
who got it from somebody in town, "They're saying
Mary Frances has a boyfriend."

People are cruel, I know that,
yet none so cruel as whatever it is
that wakes a vibrant girl
from the sleep of her empty bed

and sends her out of her empty house
into the rain and darkness,
sends her out to fight
through a labyrinth of rocks and fences,

sharp cutting things, monstrous shadows,
and crashes of lightning, this thing
that impels her finally, impossibly,
to make her way to the deeply remembered

and yearned-for other,
only to find
that in her passion
she has been changed

into a crazy
old woman
with people laughing
in her face.

CLOSING DOWN HER HOUSE

Hers because she'd lived there seventy years,
whereas at eighteen we'd left the place,
my brother and I, middle-aged men hurrying and crazy
as thieves, our wives rushed and careless,

going through her things, making stacks,
then forgetting what was in which stack,
shouting questions, "Do you want this?"
"What should I do with . . . ?" holding up

pictures, books, vases, doodads, old toys
—ah God, I'd be happy enough not to think
about that day ever again, the day I hauled
her dresser, her pie press, her grandmother's

Victorian sofa, even her brass bed frame
out and up the ramp of our rented truck,
yellow hulking thing backed up to her porch
like some awful growth the house had sprouted

now that we'd moved her to the home
in Wytheville, now that we had helped her
pick out just a few of her things to have
in her room to remind her of home.

This was a day hot enough to make my brother
and me sweat hard, me showing off my fitness-
club muscles, all of us making harsh jokes
and carrying out the brutality of that work

as if it had to be done fast or else
something terrible would happen—
but the terrible thing was happening
right there in the dusty air we breathed,

in the sacked rooms, right there in the
shell of the kitchen where she sat mornings
sipping coffee while she waited for my father
to come to breakfast, right there in the hearts

of my brother and me, who knew we had to
commit that destruction, and in the hearts
of our wives, who could see their futures
in the chaos of her rooms, her things, her

absence. . . .

I ask myself again, what was our hurry?
Why didn't we give ourselves a week
instead of two days? We could have gone
room by room, we could have honored

the thousands of hours of ordinary life
lived in those rooms. We didn't have to
desecrate the place. Some of her things
we stored in Pulaski to be picked up later,

some we just abandoned, and the rest
went to Georgia in the rented truck. Her car
we loaded onto a trailer ramp hooked
to the truck, and that whole apparatus

was comical and trashy the way it bobbed
and swayed its way out the driveway,
over her road's humps and pits. Thieves
would have claimed more dignity leaving

a place they'd plundered. The house remained
where it was, of course—where it had stood
for a hundred years—and we children ran away
from it that afternoon, but as I followed

the truck and her captured car around the last
curve where you could look back and see
an upstairs window, a roof and a chimney,
I had that queasy sense of seeing the other

thing move away while I stood still. I won't
see it again was the stab of knowledge
that came to me then. I'm glad now
that at least I could know that much.

On the interstate in our rented car,
driving south to the Greensboro airport,
my wife and I talked the whole thing out,
so that we had liberated ourselves

from what we'd gone through back there
and were ready to get back to our lives
by the time we reached the Avis station.
"Would you pop the trunk please?"

the attendant called, and I did it
absentmindedly because our luggage
was in the back seat. "You've got
some things here," he said. Disbelieving,

my wife and I walked back there to see:
a stack of framed pictures, the blue bowl
Uncle Bill had brought back from Cyprus,
a bag of odds and ends—a stash

of things my sister-in-law had meant
to move to her own car, special items
she wanted to take home with her. Now we
had it and our luggage and twenty minutes

to catch our plane. Somehow we hauled it
all into the airport, up to the ticket-line,
dragged it to the counter, begged for boxes
to pack it in, angered everybody in sight

with our mess, our sweaty disarray—I snapped
at my wife for politely explaining our problem
to the crowd. The special items flew with us
here to Vermont. Of course the blue bowl broke,

as did the glass in several picture frames,
but it's all here, with us, dispersed
around the rooms of our house,
the place where we live with our children.

A Brief History of
My Mother's Temper

1

We didn't want
to make her mad.
Formal spankings
with the hairbrush

were a justice
we understood,
but when her rage
boiled over, that

was when we knew
we'd get scalded.
Her witch's looks
felt like a slap

across the face,
but she could laugh
about them, too,
as if they were

harmless, they were
just a warning:
Stop that right now.
Not one more word.

2

When her last son
went to college,
she changed so much
our amazement

lasted for years.
"Mellow granny"
we might have called
her, except that

now and then she'd
blast a grandchild
with a forty-
watt witch's look,

and then it came
back to us, how
in the old days
we feared her rage.

3

Headstrong, fifteen
years old, she was
too beautiful
for school, for life

in that small town,
for anything
but the marriage
she demanded.

Her parents said
yes, probably
relieved to have
my father take

over the job
of raising her.
He did it by
not thwarting her.

4

Certain famous
episodes stick
with me even
now—the time she

threw the dish
drainer at Charles,
the time she said
I was ugly

when I clutched her
skirt and wouldn't
stop crying—but
the whole truth is

she wasn't an
angry person
—really—though now
it seems that way.

With each of us
she spent hours
talking quietly—
she could listen—

and she liked us.
For us to grow
up knowing that
was like having

a secret stash
of money sewn
into our shirts,
something always

there to help us
through the hard times.
As long as she
lived in that house,

I wanted to see
her, wanted to sit
with her and talk,
just sit and talk.

5

Shut up! Goddamn
it, all of you,
shut up! That was
what I woke up

hearing her shout—
it was her, but
it wasn't her.
She never cursed,

and her voice
sounded all wrong.
My brain was slow
to process it—

I'd been asleep
in my boyhood
bed, and my wife
and daughters were

downstairs talking
with my brother,
his wife, and their
sons. Then I heard

them laugh and knew
they'd waked her up—
it was maybe
midnight, a time

she considered
inappropriate
for frivolous
socializing.

She was riled up,
but the others
hadn't heard her,
and so I burst

out of bed, ran
downstairs to shush
them, then came back
up to tell her

they'd be quiet
now, she could go
back to sleep. *You
take your goddamn*

*family out
of here! Go back
where you came from!*
"All right, Mother,

we'll be quiet
now, please don't—"
*Get out! Go disturb
somebody else!*

Back in my old
bed, I listened
to the quiet
steps the others

made tiptoeing
to their rooms, their
beds. Soon my wife
was there with me,

and the house was
as quiet as it
ever had been.
Fifty years old,

I was a child
whose mother'd just
said, *Go away.*
The old promise

—I will hurt you!—
had been made good.
My wife and I
didn't even

dare whisper our
thoughts, but my plan
was to pack up
in the morning

and leave. Of course
the next morning
she cried, she begged
our forgiveness,

she was truly
pitiful. Who
was she now? Who
was this woman?

6

My brother's wife
began reading
books about it—
Alzheimer's. I

confess I'm in
denial. I
won't read, won't watch
TV programs

on it, but still
little pieces
of knowledge make
their way into

my brain. The brain
of course is what's
at issue here.
My mother is

still my mother
even if her
mind isn't her
own anymore.

I need to make
her know I love
her, even if
she says, *Get out*

and don't come back!
which is what she
did say our first
visit to her

in the nursing
home. My brother's
troubled the same
as me. We take

her words the way,
in her fury
of the moment,
she means them. What

she says echoes
back through the years
to before we
were born, to when

we were in her
womb and hearing
her voice with
our whole bodies—

if our mother
hates us, then so
does God, so does
the universe.

7

Well, that's enough
about her, let's
talk about me
for a while. I'm

in excellent
health, I've got my
family, friends,
house, job, car, dog.

My mind doesn't
play tricks on me.
My emotions
are perfectly

under control.
I'm not old, I
have a future,
I am loved.

8

We get reports
of what she does
in the home near
my brother's house.

She hit a nurse,
she cursed an aide,
and sometimes she
calls her roommate

"that nigger." Oh,
Mother, I wish . . .
Well, exactly
what do I wish

for you, for us,
for anybody
who has to go
through Alzheimer's?

Wishing is for
babies, I guess.
Blowing candles
out only works

for kids. Daylight
is what grown-ups
get. We get days
full of sunlight,

and maybe that's
all right because
it takes almost
a lifetime to

appreciate
one clear, bright day.
Mother, I wish
you this day's light.

Writing About Her

My mother would think she's Jesus Christ
if she knew how written about she is and not
just by me. Bess has set her down on paper,
too. In Bess's poems, she's a romantic

figure of stature and consequence.
Mother confessed things to Bess she never
would have told me—like sometimes walking
through the house naked after her bath. My poet

daughter set that forth with delicacy
by putting it in the context of love,
the widow's ritual of erotic grief,
the old body remembering the young body.

Molly's coming along now, writing
the occasional story for school.
Her granny hasn't shown up in them yet,
but when she does, Bess and I will just nod.

Charles, my older brother, writes mysteries
—unpublished so far, but his luck is due
to change. Anyway, Mother isn't directly
present in those manuscripts, but her biscuits

are, and so is her fried chicken, along
with some of her sayings, like "Some rain
must fall." She was fond of that one.
Not a bad saying to pass along to sons

with grand dreams and moderate talent.
Bill, my younger brother, doesn't write
—at least not in a literary way—
but here is the thing: his letters

take on energy and bite when he writes
about Mother. And he has to write about her
a fair amount nowadays since he's taken her
to the home in Georgia near his house.

So he writes about how she does at Easter
and Christmas, what meds she's taking,
and how she longs for her house in Ivanhoe.
Some of what he writes is in regular letters

and some of it is in e-mail messages.
He's bilhuddle@aol.com.
I'm dhuddle@gnu.uvt.edu.
She's Mary Frances Huddle, née Akers;

born in Dublin, Virginia, in 1919;
longtime resident of Ivanhoe, Virginia;
wife of Richard Huddle for fifty-three years;
widow; mother of three sons; grandmother

of seven; great-grandmother of two;
taxpayer; voter; Alzheimer's victim . . .
There, you see how it is? Easiest thing
in the world to put my mother into words.

Minor Suite

1

Buttermilk dough
stuck to her fingers
before she plumped it out
and cut the white circles
to set on the black iron.
Clean bowl to pan in the oven
took her about twelve minutes.

Once a day, sometimes twice,
she did this for fifty-some years.

The last months she lived
in the house and couldn't even
put a pot on a burner without
forgetting it, she still made
biscuits so perfect
you'd eat three or four
before you could stop.

2

At playing cards,
sewing, swimming,
witty conversation,
talking politics,
driving a car,
singing in church,
and keeping house,
her talent was average
or a little below.

So what
was she good at?

Being
who she was:
Mary Frances Huddle
from Ivanhoe, Virginia,
somebody who lived
in a white house
on a hill
way out
in the country.

3

She practiced a certain decorum
when she went somewhere:
even in jeans, loafers,
and her oldest blouse,
she still combed her hair
and put on lipstick before
she drove down to Price's Store.
Parked down there one afternoon,

she and I saw Mrs. Perkins flying
down Church Hill on Toby's bicycle,
face red, hair wild, and skirt up
to her thighs. "Ran out of beer,"
Mrs. P. shouted, gliding past us
on her way to Gracey's, the one place
in town that had a license. "That woman,"
my mother said, tight-lipped
and grim. "That woman."

4

Always up early,
she put the coffee on
then went to the fireplace,
shoveled out the ashes,
and set paper and kindling
atop the dying coals.

Unless you were family
you never saw her like this,
squatting on the hearth,
Neanderthal,
facing those first
tongues of flame.

NEVER BEEN

In the place where I have never been,
a dreamed white horse with thudding hooves
carries me through fern-scented woods
to a hilltop meadow where they wait for me,
my young father and mother, my brothers
as boys again, Lindsey, the wife I am meeting
that first night in Charlottesville, and Bess
and Molly, our daughters just as they are today.

In the place where I have never been,
we arrange white linen on the grass. For hours
we feast and talk with each other, then play
croquet on the finely mown and rolled court.
Charles teases our father, and we are all
the hilarious, bawdy, and brilliant players.
Our one intricate game continues through
the afternoon while the light slowly deepens.

In the place where I have never been,
this is the time of day when the old ones
appear, sitting in their chairs nearby—
Grandmama and Granddad, Aunt Stella and Gran,
Uncle Bo and Aunt Iva, even Grandma Lawson,
still gumming snuff and grinning guiltily.
These ancient ones go on with their stories,
using the manners of that earlier time

when this place where I have never been was
the dream set into our minds, the vision
of a happiness that was possible and correct,
a green and sunlit valley opening before
my brothers and me as we grew to adulthood,
as we took jobs, married, fathered children,
bought houses, and settled into patterns
that would become our lives, our proper lives.

This place my brothers and I have never been
was reason enough to try to be honest men,
men who work hard, accept responsibility,
and speak and act with manly forthrightness.
We would be rewarded. We would go to bed
on clean linen, sleep deeply through the night,
and wake to loving wives and children, sunny days,
and good work to be done. When pain came to us,

in this place I have never been, it wouldn't
last, it wouldn't be pain a man couldn't defeat
through strength of character. The vision
of that sunlit hilltop meadow where family
always waited to welcome us was what my brothers
and I held deeply in mind through all our days
as students, soldiers, husbands, and fathers,
as men carrying on the work of the world.

The place is out of reach. I'm about to be
old, and it's farther away than it ever was—
no meadow, no sunlight, family dispersed by time,
madness, alcohol, and death. The old ones sleep
so soundly they cannot be awakened. I confess
to failures of love, truth, and decency. I know
it is my fault I can't find my way to the beloved
place where green grass is graced with white linen,

where food and laughter and loved ones wait.
Justice requires me never
to reach the destination toward which my entire life
was directed. I can't really argue. It's just
that now my daughters
are moving toward the place I can't help but promise them,
the green meadow shining
in sunlight. And that is where I wait for them, arms extended.

So Long

Pets of my childhood and our white house
with the dandelioned yard, bordered by locust trees,
sassafras, and wild cherry always swaying in the wind
of our hill—of course lilacs and of course forsythia
in spring, wild strawberries in summer, who would not
want all this? Blackberries along the path through the fields
to muddy New River, with its mountain of cool forest rising
from the opposite bank. June bugs, honeysuckle, my funny
grandfather who could set the broken arm of a cat;
my mother and father, my brothers, the cedary smell
of Christmas morning with candlelight and cold stair-steps
on three boys' bare feet.

My mother's mind
is dissolving now, my father is eight years dead,
Aunt Iva dead two weeks after Uncle Bo,
Gran and Grandmama both long gone,
my grandfather's house burnt
to the ground.

To what end do I hold on to this
little boat packed up with days and voices,
hands, sunlight, birdsong, the ten thousand
fragrances of a single moment? I want to let it
drift away. . . .

Last visit
to Mother's house we began opening cabinets
and drawers to look for photographs. They came out—
snapshots, portraits, bodies, and faces
spattering randomly across the years—
                              We could have tossed them
across the floor and furniture, we could have
walked and sat on them, set glasses and plates on them,
and we did make rather a mess of them on the coffee table.
At the end, though, after some quarreling
over which cousins got which pictures, we put most of them back,
packed up the others and brought them into our homes,
mine in Vermont, my brother's in Georgia. . . .

                                        What holds me
out of time now: indignation over the loss
of my mother and Aunt Murrell sunning their legs
on the back porch steps, anger that my father's
brilliant youth became in a blink of God's eye
his slow death by emphysema, sorrow that my brother
Charles and I can't talk any more.

                          I know a place
on the New Haven River
where I caught a fair-sized trout once,
caught it clean
out of a fast riffle against the far bank
with a nymph tied by hand by my friend John Engels,
and though I wanted to carry that rainbow
downstream to show it to John,
for some reason I didn't understand then
and don't understand now,

I put it back,
wet my hand to grasp the fish behind its gills,
took the hook out of its lip,
then bent to the cold water
to let it slip back,
alive. . . .

Son of a bitch God

Whose left hand fires tonight's sunset

over Lake Champlain and Whose right

sends a child in Sarajevo into a hail of gunfire,

Who let me sing Rose, Rose I Love You

in the car with my brothers and my parents

on the way to Hester's Drive-In

to see *High Noon*,

Who then tortured my father to death,

and Who now means

to drag my mother down into insanity,

I know better
than to pray for help knowing the whole of what
for a few moments of a sunny afternoon fishing
the New Haven River I must have known
a small part,

how to let go—

my mother cooking supper

my father whistling as he walked home from work